A BETTY LOU MURDER MYSTERY COMEDY, SHERIFF NATHAN BOTTOM MEETS CHUPACABRA

Series 2 illustrated

Keith Hulse

Dedicated to lovers of a good laugh,
to lovers of the fun stuff,
the ridiculous,
the slap stick,
the comedy mayhem,
to comedy riot.

CONTENTS

A BETTY LOU MURDER MYSTERY COMEDY, SHERIFF BOTTOM MEETS CHUPACABRA

2nd Adventure

Illustrated

BY

Keith Hulse

55587 words 241 pages

Keith Hulse

Aberdeen

Lugbooks@gmail.com

Lugbooks.co.uk

[CHAPTER 1] — MEET AGAIN

Terlingua population 127

"Well Sheriff we are in Texas, bet you would like to visit your mum and dad Nathan," Deputy Clay Eagle asked his friend and boss.

"Friend Clay we are here to investigate the Chupacabra not my ancestry," Nathan pulling rank and of course Clay not only went into the huffs, but was tempted to say, "You told everyone you were raised in Texas, but your ex-girlfriend who was my ex-girlfriend Madam Medium Wendy Lou who was seeing us both for *cooking lessons in how to cook perfect Texan Refried Beans*, told me you confided in her you were a New York orphan, unloved and never adopted because you was on the shrimp size," but Clay was a pacifist, kindly in nature, never hurt a fly type of guy so we ask, *"Why are you a lawman giggle?"* **It is a secret so do not ask.**

*"A giggle, who is the giggle, it is not a secret and is revealed shortly giggle."

And as they rested on their horses, Nathan Bottom's

magnificent black mare, a nice and gentle horse so there was no risk of being jettisoned onto a cacti, an easy thing for a horse to do since the sheriff seemed to have stopped growing as a child, so really was unable to control the shiny black coated animal, and why he now and again dropped a hand with a sugar lump to the horse's mouth.

"Manni, that horse will be a diabetic before we get to "Terlingua," Clay forgetting Nathan was his boss because **they were best of friends.**

"Bray," Clay's palomino horse, as he was the Native American side kick, slap stick comedian and all-round stunt and fun character, handsome, well-built, always in leopard print 'Y's and the opposite of Nathan who was serious and believed he walked in the footsteps of Sherlock Holmes even if he was allergic to pipe smoke. He was also the reincarnation of Wild Bill the famous lawman who was shot in the back of the head so Nathan might exit this world same way soon and then you can go read Moby Dick the classic instead of this ridiculous tale about Texas where everything is big.

"Hiss," a rattler and Diamond Back Rattlers are bigger than those these men met in their last job, in Alaska where they met Big Foot.

"S**t it sprang onto me Nathan, save me friend," Sheriff Bottom fussing his hands in the air.

Clay watched the big snake slither into the grass before he edged his palomino against Nathan's mare.

An evil glint sparkled in the palomino's eyes; the horse was a Horney stallion which means *"cooking lessons again."*

"All safe boss," Nathan throwing away the small tumble weed that had entangled itself on Nathan his sheriff.

Sheriff Nathan looked down, rubbed his chin with a hand, "It will be **our secret Friend.**"

"Sure, thing best friend," Clay and they tottered forward to town the best of friends, while it lasted.

Then the horses sprinted as the mare knew the palomino was interested, the mare was a flirt, not even in heat, just high on sugar cubes.

"Clay, you're the F*****g Native American, what the heck do we do?" Sheriff Nathan with free hands thinking of following the image he had in his head, of a circus act, a scantily dressed female standing on a white horse about to jump through a flaming hoop, and a second before it did, she jumped onto a passing horse, caught by a semi naked man in a big cod piece and skintight pantaloons that had ripped as they had shrunk in the wash.

Silence greeted Nathan and he should not have copied his vision before checking if Clay was near him. Well, the palomino's head was, **but that did not mean anything.**

Had Nathan forgotten Clay was an Alaskan Native American Indian, someone who fished salmon, smoked, and ate it by cold clear rivers. A man who was more comfortable trekking mountain trails than a Comanche Native American, born and schooled on a horse to do everything on a horse like the ancient Scythians, *"Do not ask".*

"And was all hype, Clay was a modern Native American who used combustion engines to travel and supermarket salmon to buy giggle."

And Sheriff Nathan jumped, "Catch me best friend."

"Thud," the sound of Nathan hitting Pan Handle dust.

"Better get up quick Sheriff, this place is crawling with rattlers," and, **"this is our secret** best friend, Nathan."

And Nathan rose and pointed at two vanishing horses visibly enjoying their freedom with the palomino obviously trying it on horse fashion.

"Bray," and "bray," the mules with their food, tents, six

shooters and vet tranquilizer gun behind them.

Then the mules ran off after the horses.

"The f******g s***s," Clay knowing exactly what the horses and mules were.

"Dargah," Nathan throwing his ten-gallon brown cowboy hat down and stamping on it.

"We got to walk in these cowboy boots," Clay and mentally began blaming Sheriff Nathan Bottom for wanting to ride into town like the Lone Ranger and Tonto, be hailed heroes before they done anything to be called 'heroes,' while four wheeled trek bikes were available and did any of them check if the mules were a boy and girl donkey? Maybe they were Shetland ponies and not mules, **did they check**, no.

"See that smudge on the horizon Deputy Clay, that is Terlingua," and Nathan followed the horses.

Deputy Clay knew just like before, they were no longer **'best friends,'** and wondered if Nathan had an accident out here, like standing on a rattler, did they blame him.

* *"It was a long walk to town and a hot day, and they had no water so did not have to worry about needing a latrine, giggle, girly joke, and loved the way Nathan jumped horses, a true man with 'True Grit,' but an* idiot *for not looking first, and that is why it is hard to hate the shrimp, and yes who am I, his guide Betty Lou, the same from Alaska where I drove everyone bananas, especially my side kick Fili Pek, the Polish murdered gold panner whom I did like to murder again as he is really annoying.*

And here we go again, guiding these two hapless humans on their search for immortality amongst the clouds, and I know my Boss above me cannot bring hate towards them, they are adorable cuddly idiots deserving places as clay figurines on your mantel piece.

"I am Betty Lou the storyteller as well as spirit guide to stop them being bitten by rattlers, shot up by badmen, chased by a lynch mob, so they never have to ask from a hospital bed, where was my guardian angel, are we not supposed to have spirit guides to stop me full of XXX falling into the canal and waking up in this other dark freezing void, and what is that, that thing with a forked tail and horns coming my way, oh dear it is my deputy Clay Eagle in Halloween dress?

Your time buddy."

Anyway

"Well Rodeo King looks like another zipped open Silver Dollar cow?" Modern Cowboy Jesse said swigging fizzy caramel drink from a flask-, "our devil dogs are doing their work, looks like all the blood sucked out of the cow too."

"There is a fifty-thousand-dollar reward put up by the newspapers of this County and I intend to get it for producing **our** expendable Chupacabras that is killing their cattle, and go Nationwide on television and be famous, they are like rabbits, one will not be missed, will give them Dolly Chupacabra," Rodeo King wiping his face of sweat with his smelly red bandana and then with the other hand waved biting bugs off his face with his black Stetson, and this is Texas so the biting bugs are bigger than yours.

His eyes clouded over with vision.

"Yeh, of money, Las Vegas, swimming pools and women," Jesse peeking into Rodeo King's vision.

Silence of the Pan Handle broken by a whistle of stillness that made both men shiver and think of town and latrines, burgers, XXX, pool tables and Line Dancing at the Purple Haze where the badmen hung out playing poker, eating chili beans, drinking XXX, and ignoring the serving girls who fawned upon them and that is what the badmen were here for, to be fawned upon so spent their swag to be fawned upon, nothing else, nothing going on in the outhouse apart from mating flies, nothing upstairs as only the drunk badmen slept there, as no serving girl did lie on those bed bug infested beds, and Texan bed bugs are big.

They had brains the girls and knew it was time to fleece the drunks and blame that badman who rode out of town earlier on his trek bike.

"I hear they are bringing in two famous lawmen to solve these Chupacabra killings, well no out of state F.B.I. agents going to steal my vision," Rodeo King and put his right boot atop a dung beetle and squashed.

NOT TO WORRY, the dung beetle was smart and vamoosed out the boot gap but left the meal behind.

Rodeo King began rubbing his boot against the baked dirt to clean the meal off.

Jesse curled his nose and looked the other way and silently moved and saw clouds of dirt coming their way.

He took a long swallow of his caramel fizzy drink; it was kept cool in a cold bag in his rucksack shaped like a rattler's head, see he was a badman who advertised it with his rucksack, so you got off the sidewalk as he came by, unless you were the law, then **he** walked amongst the whatever on High Street adobe Texan towns.

Rodeo King lengthened a pocket telescope and looked.

"Horses, donkeys, no one else, think we going to be rich," Rodeo King and "*I was aghast, Fili Pek come here and save our boys,*

Fili Pek where art thou, typical lazy man never comes."

These two men walked back to their trek bikes; 'DD' gold lettering on the bikes, they were modern cowboys.

Rodeo King took a last cleaning effort of his boot before mounting.

And they were off.

Anyway.

"Listen Nathan, engines," Clay sweating much as he carried his friend on his back.

Not only had he watched the film, 'True Grit,' he was acting it for he had 'TRUE GRIT.'

Well, it was hot and those mule hybrid donkeys Shetland Ponies had cleared off with the water, shrimp flavored crisps, peanut chocolate bars and soft loo paper.

And shows even with all the "I am no longer best friend," they were, and Clay like any other person should have dumped the extra weight and said, "I will be back with help," but he did not, he carried his friend breaking the trend.

"Epee," a moan from Nathan.

Anyway.

"Martha Lou, listen and look," an elderly cowboy, "and he was a cowboy as wore a cowboy hat, a sweaty scarf about the neck, a denim shirt open to show his pulps and hairs.

"Bray," a real horse sound as Martha Lou edged her white mare closer to the man in tight denim jeans and cowboy heeled boots that gave the man extra height and blisters when walked a distance.

Thank God no spurs.

"Small tornado coming," Martha and puffed on a vape, Texan

longhorn jerky flavor as she was in the process of **trying** stopping smoking.

A packet of cigarettes with a desert animal emblem showed from a breast pocket. The packet was open, there were cigarettes missing, and her denim cleavage was open to. As blossoming as a famous blonde country and *western* singer, and still upfront for show.

"She was saying, "I got these, bet you want to see *more Mister, well guess what Bye Fili Pek, I mean jerk, giggle,"* OUR biased female guide.

She sat man style on her stunning white horse that just pooped because it was a horse.

Straightaway dung beetles emerged from holes like the ground been opened to Zombies.

"No Martha to the right of the dust cloud, that is 'DD' boys on our land and going fast, ah ha, heading for those horses and pack mules, and let me see, yep, city folk also."

Martha Lou from her cleavage retrieved a fold down telescope and looked.

The male cowboy took the opportunity to ogle her cleavage, she was a fine woman, unfortunately she did not like him the same way he liked her.

Martha stuffed the telescope back in her cleavage somewhere amongst the bandages, anti-septic wipes, tetanus jabs and snake bite remedies.

She then drew a semi-automatic rifle from where it was kept, in the cleavage? No, from a saddle scabbard.

"Boom, boom, boom," she fired into the direction of the 'DD' men. They were trespassing and she knew Rodeo King who deserved thrown down a dry well and left there for the rains.

Rodeo King was a suspect in many mysterious folk vanishings and always had a good excuse why he "found the victims red lighter on Highway 20, you detectives stop on

Highway 20 for who knows what, well I got to stop to for the same and find this lighter."

"Pity do not see any Chupacabra or that did truly pin him to all the killings," the man continued and waited till his female companion scabbarded her rifle before going forward.

AND:

"Zing," went a bullet and made Rodeo King hide underneath his Stetson, but the hat was too small for him.

"Damn my cigar," Jesse seeing how close the second "ZING," came to blowing away his pretty nose all the lying barmaids in his watering hole the Purple Haze said he had.

"Well, I am having a close look and looks bulbous and full of black heads, then I am bias giggle," Betty Lou waving at you and gave the startled man some help to fall sideways off his trek bike.

"That is my friend, go away spirit girl," and was a dark imp dislodged from Jesse's shoulder complaining about me.

"ZING PLUNK FIZZ," the third bullet inside Jesse's rucksack and caramel drink fizzed out the open rucksack top spraying Rodeo King.

Who went mental.

They were friends, but badmen do not have friends and Rodeo King swatted Jesse heaps with his Stetson.

Then the black mare and palomino knocked into them 'NEIGHING,' and being playful animals danced gently about the two cowboys swishing their tails onto people's annoyed faces.

Being drivers of polluting engine trek vehicles, the men were not impressed and forgot horses were like people, wanting attention and like elephants remembering folk who treated them as flies with their Stetsons.

"My forty-dollar Stetson, give me it back," Rodeo King but the black mare was galloping towards Terlingua where she smelt humans, and better still, water troughs and hay and she had a toy in her mouth to shred.

Jesse did not say a word, he thought better not to move also as the palomino kissed his lips and swallowed what remained of the blasted cigar.

"This horse has strange eating habits.

Then lifted its tail and peed all over Rodeo King and did not wait for the human's reaction which was guaranteed to be violent. Horses got to pee you know giggle."

"Where is my assault rifle?" Rodeo King rummaging here and there in his trek's back basket for it. It was obvious it was not sticking out, but then the man did not want it showing and explains why he took out a barrel, then looked for other parts to assemble the weapon.

*"Wonder why, SPIRIT knows all, so cannot tell you as **IS A SECRET**."*

Then the donkey whatever ran through the two cowboys knocking the men together.

Rodeo King glared down into the eyes of Jesse then threw him off and Jesse landed on donkey c**p, donkeys like horses do that too.

Jesse knowing Rodeo King really loved him as his best friend screamed bad language then jumped Rodeo King to show off, he was a tough guy, suitable to be a friend of Rodeo King his best friend, *"the idiot,"* me well he must be because,

Rodeo King beat the donkey cp out of Jesse."**

And because the two badmen were fighting, or better, one badman killing another badman never noticed two hapless lawmen near them.

"Water for my friend here," Clay dropping Nathan to the hard dirt that brought the sheriffs spirit back to activity.

Hurriedly Nathan stood wiping the dust off his navy-blue pin stripe trousers that were tucked into fake P.V.C. leather knee high fake boots. Clays vegetarian habits were rubbing off onto Nathan.

The two cowboys opposite wondered what hell had sent them for treats and their smiles faded when they saw the glint of a badge stuck on a ten-gallon hat.

Then noticed the Native American had his law badge on his belt buckle.

Jesse put a restraining hand on Rodeo King's shoulder.

"Are you Sheriff Bottom and Tonto?" Jesse informing Rodeo King why he had gripped his shoulder. Jesse was lucky, in normal circumstances Rodeo king flicked Jesse's hand off as an annoying leprous fly. He did not hold his companion in the same esteem as Jesse held him.

"Why he was King of Rodeos staying on bronco horses and bulls, enjoying the rip in his jeans as he showed off his unmentionable underwear to the girl fans screaming at him over a stain there. And he never heard because the rodeo broadcaster has his microphone on full blast, shame, giggle.

Jesse hero worshipped the fink, that reminds me where is my fink, oh Fili Pek come here giggle."

Now Clay was used to Native American taunts and smiled, **the smile of a bigger man in physical build than Rodeo King who recognized that**, so behaved, *a little bit.*

"I am and who do I not have the pleasure in meeting," for Sheriff Bottom had ears to hear and had heard 'TONTO,' to describe his best friend when it suited Clay to be his best friend.

Rodeo King **looked** the small man up and down, and because there was more ten-gallon hat than man, the looking did not take long.

"You got no side arms sheriff, this is a big state, more dirt than folks," Rodeo King when he should have said, "Welcome boys, lost your horses, never mind, hop aboard, soon have you drinking black hot coffee and eating refried beans."

Jesse knew Rodeo King could beat up the Native American,

he beat up Latinos weekends when drunk, and Native Americans were just Latinos who should be sent back to Mexico.

"Guess you are here to find out if the Chupacabra is real?" Rodeo King not wanting the lawmen **to find out anything**, he did not like lawmen but did like unarmed lawmen.

Rodeo King threw a right hook, South Paw fashion at Clay who jumped back allowing a shrimp to land a cowboy P.V.C. boot on the man's chin.

Rodeo king counted rattlesnakes, bronco animals and barmaids dancing line to western music.

Jesse looked from his fallen friend to our heroes and from nowhere flashed a bowie knife with these words, "No one hits my friend."

"I did," the little sheriff and high kicked him in the important place so Jesse collapsed to his knees where Clay easily handcuffed him.

Nathan gave Clay cuffs for the senseless man lying amongst donkey c**p and scuttling dung beetles and a pair of nurse's rubber gloves to keep his hands sparkling clean.

"Cool drink **best friend** Nathan," Clay having opened a rucksack.

"Why thank you **friend best** Clay," and both men drank knowing they did not have to walk into Terlingua but drive in as HEROES.

"They knew from experience men like these two were bullies and folks said 'Hello,' to their faces and gave them the sidewalk and as soon as passed, "farts," said in a whisper. Yes, now the 'windbags' could be said louder, Sheriff Nathan Bottom and Deputy Clay Eagle were in town.

Character Update Sheriff Nathan Bottom one of the two lawmen heroes from the tales of 'Big Foot, A Betty Lou Sheriff

Bottom Murder Mystery Comedy,' the other being Deputy Clay Eagle.

What had made Sheriff Bottom to aspire to be an unloved lawman? Well he set out to be a loved lawman, respected, people offering the morning coffee doughnuts as he passed, dogs wagging their tails and licking his boots to a high polish, the girls fawning on the sidewalk offering themselves up as a carpet, but it all went wrong, he stopped growing as stopped eating his 'Green Giant' greens, drinking milk, and reading comics, he became serious watching 'Lone Ranger remakes, and knew he needed a Tonto, a side kick to take the blame for his mistakes for Nathan came last in the Police Academy so was kicked out.

He simply put an ad out and Clay answered and believed and started calling himself Deputy Clay Eagle.

What did Nathan call himself, why Sheriff Nathan Bottom and together the two went cryptid hunting as realized that was the way to television fame, Cadillac's, many divorces and dime a dozen pulp fiction written on them, **but they did beloved.**

So was the desire to be loved that pushed Sheriff Nathan Bottom on, to be patted instead of a dog next to him outside an ice cream parlor, he was human.

And bought a ten-gallon hat and pin stripes and looked a miniature western lawman of by gone days.

Bought a ticket to Alaska where he found Big Foot and solve the Betty Lou Murders and when he walked down the Amtrak train, people noticed the tall handsome deputy behind him carrying the luggage.

Would Sheriff Nathan Bottom ever find human affection, a hug or two, a doughnut, a seat, never, he was so small no one noticed till the ten-gallon hat passed.

Update Giggles

"Betty Lou is my name and ride the clouds above and skii the rainbows and annoy my angelic bosses.

In my appointment as spirit guide to Nathan Bottom I failed miserably in the last adventure chasing Big Foot in Alaska, so was sent back to prove my self a second time a worthy guide, as my bosses are kind and obviously not caring or did give me an easy subject, someone who licks ice cream cones, eats sugary doughnuts breakfast, lunch and dinner, spends free time on a game console drinking fizzy drinks and eating more sugary doughnuts

A safe task with no danger apart from losing a game.

Not a lawman who faces down gunslingers and holds up a stop sign to stampeding cows. A man who walks miles without food, a small man under a ten-gallon hat with a sheriff badge pinned on it.

I am doomed to fail again."

[CHAPTER 2] — HELO AND WELCOME

Martha carried guns and used them.

The trouble was that first dent indentation in the dusty soil was Sheriff Bottom who silently violently left the trek that ran on petrol not sugar cubes.

Truly a man of True Grit as never moaned.

"Friend are you alright," Deputy Clay dismounting and showing intuition, turned off the trek, *just in case it went the way of the horses.*

"Well, howdy boys," Martha said behind Clay and she and her cowboy friend had been so quiet in their approach, Clay clutched his chest **in horror movie surprise.**

It was her cowhand Kit, that dismounted and helped Clay retrieve Nathan and dust him down with big solid hand whacks, so Nathan made funny faces each time he was dusted.

"I am Big Martha Lou of the Silver Dollar Ranch and Mercury Mine over in McCamey County and see you have collared two skunks."

"Big Martha you do not do anything unlawful to me as these are lawmen," Rodeo King afraid Big Martha would dispense her type of Texas justice on him.

"I know who these boys are, and I will hang you one day for rustling when I catch you red handed," Big Martha replied a tower of a woman upon her horse looking down at the tussled up bad men who looking up sneered as they had ogled a knee, a slit denim riding dress, and those appendages sticking from Martha's chest where a good cowgirl on the range kept what a girl on the range needed, mobile phone, tin opener, black book, lucky wooly gopher feet, change of elastics and much more but that **is a girls secret**.

"I thought you were untying me," Jesse implored to the cowhand Kit, so much laughter followed from him and Big Martha who together from nowhere tore at jerky, *snapping turtle flavor*, gave a quick chew, then spat the disgusting mess at the two badmen.

Believe me it was disgusting.

Yes, Terlingua was on the horizon, a FAR AWAY TOWN twinkling cold fizzy caramel drinks, double cheeseburgers with French Fries, they had to get there as eating all those carbohydrates found in Rodeo King's rucksacks causes reflex and unexpected bowel movements.

What unexpected carbohydrates do you really want to know?

*

"Here I am oh beautiful one, have I missed anything?" Fili Pek my spiritual helper **being sarcastic** and coming from Spirit in a flash knew the past and present here as Spirit knows ALL.

"Make sure the badmen do not get free," I told him, puckered the red transparent lips, and made disgusting kissing sounds

as knew Fili Pek was in love with me as I was a beautiful spirit woman whom he adored as I am so adorable.

There was a worldly sigh from his direction.

"Oh, look a white butterfly," Big Martha seeing Fili Pek's orb float down to the badmen.

Now that was something, she was physic, *"Hello I am Betty Lou can you hear me?"* But no, not that physic but beware lady, having physic gifts brings all sorts of unwanted spirits attracted to you, like that Fili Pek who thinks he is every woman's desire, the fink, *"giggle,"* repeatedly as know being cruel to Fili Pek is what Fili Pek craves for, my attention.

But he deserves it, his ancestors were slimy worms found on seashores, pepper, and vinegar because he is a MALE spirit.

"I had forgotten all my lessons from the Alaskan Big Foot adventure, so must sigh and look sad, repentant, be remorseful and not mean any of the blah, just cannot help myself when Fili Pek is near."

Anyway: having two roped badmen on the back of bouncing treks was courting disaster.

It happened thus.

1] The horses came back neighing looking for sugar cubes so cramped

Sheriff Nathan's trek handling style, they knew sugar cubes were in his pockets so stuck their snouts there knocking Nathan off again covering him in foot long horse sticky saliva.

It happened thus.

2] The donkeys followed the horses and knew what was good for the horses was good for them, so had a go at Nathan's other pockets, all his pockets so he was a desperate man crawling under his trek with four-foot equine saliva trailing from his moons.

"That shrimp lawman is arresting me," and Rodeo

king laughed like a walrus so was more the sound of bad wind than a joyful laugh for bad men laughs like CHUPACABRA crossed with hyenas, a jackal or two and Rodeo King's mother.

Jesse laughed and folk looked for a parrot escaped from Houston Zoo as parrots are good at imitating.

It happened thus.

3] Dust choked them almost dead, well four of them anyway. Two badmen who could not use their hands to cover their breathing bits with their bandanas, and two lawmen used to snow and ice so did not have western big Texan bandanas.

So, when the dust settled the four men looked like aliens so only the eyes showed, all else was **red dust.**

It took five minutes for these men to stop coughing and think again about eating their jerky Condor flavor buns with chili gherkins covered in hottest chili refried beans, cold fizzy caramel drinks produced from nowhere, just where did that food come from, a **SECRET** ok? And spat out beans and barbecued longhorn flavored chewing gum ready to speak, after wiping the mouths with hands covered in steel gloves made to pull down barbed wire.

"For an instant looked like their lips had been wiped away. Those men must have had gorilla fingers to move those hardened gloves, except for Martha's that were soft worked deer skin as was a lady like me, giggle.

Do you really think a rich pretty woman like Martha did do grubby range work? Of course not, she paid you to get bitten by water moccasins, rattlers and BIG TEXAN wasps and eat hottest chili refried beans stale flavor as you worked her range for three months, giggle, and came back to the bunk house INSANE.

Money counts and having big 48D appendages that men worshipped and rode the range for three months just to come back for an ogle, and that kept them INSANE.

But never ogled again as a white van came silently in the night and took the INSANE away to be locked up somewhere in BIG Texas.

Never mind, the medical bill came out of their wages as when they were better, had to return to work to pay for that.

So, Martha was happy, she did not have to give repeated job interviews, she had her cowboys."

From Sheriff Bottom's lowly eye level, remember he was on the dirt, he saw many extra horse hooves, some idle others pawing the ground making him cross eyed, they could smell horse stuff all over him and knew he had to get to his rucksack and sugar cubes for them.

It happened thus.

4] There was the sound of a lot of weapons clicking as guns left safety.

"Nathan, I see a white Tonka coming for me in the sky," Clay told Nathan who knew from experience that when his friend spoke thus, things were bad. Yes, things were as a lot of those guns were pointed at them.

"We want Rodeo King or else?" The lead cowboy of the now obvious arrived badman pack said.

"Rattle."

"Everyone looked down for a big diamond back and saw none but the rattling kept up to spook the horses."

"I am dying and going eat every horse here," a much wide-open eyed Rodeo King being visionary as the spooked horses hooved and pawed anything below them *including* him, just missing places.

"I will be in heaven with you Rodeo King," Jesse displaying mental health problems.

"You got a minute to vamoose or be blasted to hell cowgirls," Martha insulting the new badmen.

"Clay, I do not know where my watch is, those snouts ate it," a worried Nathan.

"Rattle," repeatedly and a gun went off.

"Think I am hit friend Nathan, Tonka is here, gasp I cannot breathe, bye friend," Clay Eagle holding a donkey across his body.

"What a bunch of lousy sharp shooters, all missed, thank Spirit, no giggles just a spiritual phew."

"Stop this madness and help me get this donkey of Clay and take your lawless friends, always another time to arrest them, a Saturday night perhaps?" Nathan finding his sugar cubes and enticing the **terrified** donkey off his **best** friend.

"I can breathe, where did Tonka go?" Clay asked.

"Someone shoots the Native American," an unknown bad man.

"My what wisdom you have sheriff," Martha impressed by Nathan and knew he was right, Rodeo King did get drunk in town weekend looking for his 'Purple Haze Bar," in the Latin quarter of town, a bar full of 'PURPLE HAZE,' girls pushing tequila with a drowned worm and slice of lime in the glass and the girls hoping for a game of private poker and *cooking lessons in Guatemala refried beans upstairs.*

Yes Sir the Purple Haze was full of lawless men and Martha knew they had met their match in Sheriff Nathan Bottom.

"I think she fancied him or was full of gas releasing refried beans, giggle."

The cowhand with Martha already down cut the badmen free, no one untied knots not when you had a chance to show off knife handles with a silver bar as the handle, others embedded with Aztec looted gems and gold, even teeth with gold fillings *to be different.*

Kit's knife handle had a picture of Sam Houston on it, worn away almost by handling, but to a Texan honorably identifiable.

It happened thus.

4] Rodeo King was unappreciative of Sheriff Nathan's kindness in stopping the gun fight, for he lurched at Nathan, but the donkeys had gnawed the top button of his Levi Denim Jeans, so they entangled him about the ankles.

"Pink?" Martha gasped.

"Teddy bear print," her cowhand Kit and all laughed, even the badmen on horses but not if the good folk for they were not supposed to laugh over their Boss's discomfort.

"Maybe there were aspirers amongst them to be BOSS of the Bad Men and must hate Rodeo King, an easy thing to do so had forgotten 'Love thy Enemy. And I love you Fili Pek and was a lie.

Now Fili Pek my helper was holding a rattler making 'rattle' sounds amongst the badmen. He was holding Clay's spirit guide, 'Snake Rattle.'

My Fili Pek does not need telling what to do."

"I will save you, Boss," *and was not Fili Pek crawling about my ankles but Jesse, who helped Rodeo King to a mounted horse, where a badman took his hand and let his horse run from 'RATTLE,' snake sounds.*

The men of the SD all laughed, and Martha lit a cheroot and plucked off Nathan's ten-gallon hat and had a good look at what she admired, Nathan gazed back with puppy dog eyes that did melt an iceberg, and did, Martha grinned with eyes all glazed, IT WAS SICKENING.

Martha put Nathan's hat back and looked intently at Clay Eagle, **now I was jealous***, that magnificent looking man* was mine.

"Smoke," she offered Clay meaning a lot for she desired him to share her cheroot, where her lips had been, and his could before she puffed again.

Silence amongst her cowhands, and one, the original cowhand Kit was not amused Martha was offering Clay her 'barbecued steaks and refried beans Texan Style flavored cheroot.

"Sorry mam, I do not smoke," Clay and sorted Nathan out on his trek advising him to drive slowly.

Martha, well her eyes mirrored the opposite humor in the eyes of her men. Clay was a challenge, she liked challenges, and Nathan could be her lap dog, she was glad she had sent for these lawmen to clear the area of Chupacabra.

That made her wonder if the lawmen were fit for the job, why Nathan could not ride a trek or horse and Clay was simply to good looking to be exposed to violence.

Clay unzipped and tucked in his brown deputy shirt exposing regulation blue deputy underwear.

Martha did not inhale but let the smoke crawl out her nose which gave her a bad sneezing fit, so she saw nothing else, *"what a shame."*

When she cleared her vision, the lawmen were a hundred yards ahead going to Terlingua.

"Come on boys," Martha shouted and got her horse galloping.

"Are we going to die Clay, do you see Tonka again?" Nathan asked as the soil thundered under the trek bikes.

Clay did not answer, the prettiest thing he ever seen was in front of him driving a 4x4 pick up. Somehow, he did keep this girl to himself, Martha could have Nathan as a boyfriend teaching Nathan to play dead, wag his moons for Texan Bison flavor biscuit and then they did always be best friends.

Trouble was, Martha saw the prettiest thing ever created to, and infuriated made her horsemen gallop about the 4x4.

"Judas priest, whoever she was, Martha was no better than

the Rodeo King, power and horse manure had gone to her brains, giggle."

"Just put your treks in the back of my pickup and we will be in Terlingua no time," the prettiest thing created said and Clay did nothing as his bottom had taking over his thinking, he was mesmerized male fashion, **it was alright, Chelsea was chirping sweetly.**

And because Martha represented the good guys did not fill the pretty thing full of holes as Rodeo King did have done, sorry, he did have kidnapped her **and she be never seen again.**

Rodeo King was suspect in many crimes but never arrested, why, **it is a secret that is why.**

Martha did not tell her men to help but all twenty of them did, stepping on toes, deliberately bumping another away, cussing and all to impress the 'Prettiest Thing Created.'

"Hi there Chelsea Lou," was repeated twenty times, Martha wanted to **'puke.'**

Then this ugly critter ran amongst them, so the horses reared and bolted chased by a mangy looking jackal looking animal that had a spiny back.

A name tag was about the neck, with good eyesight you could read, 'DOLLY.'

"That is what you get for ogling, now go get those horses and shoot to kill," Martha and the boys understood, the Chupacabra had just spooked their mounts to suck their blood later with refried beans Pecan Pie Flavor, after all, it was from Texas.

"Now is your chance boys, I want that Chupacabra stuffed above my ranch entrance gates," Martha and flicked the cheroot away then realized the new lawmen were unarmed.

Then she smiled, Clay was putting on ivory handled colts, straight out of a museum.

"**What is that?**" She asked Nathan.

"Tranquilizer guns," and gave his lost puppy dog look and Martha knew she had to adopt him and ride with him this day or he did be Chupacabra pooh.

"Vroom cough splutter," the trek bikes and went nowhere as out of fuel.

"Push the treks aboard, then we give chase," the Prettiest Thing Created and from nowhere was hugging an army heavy machine gun and bandoleer straight out of the AA Team film set.

Clay wanted back in Alaska where women kept spare keys in garters not army spares.

Nathan wanted Medium Wendy Lou back in his life and the remains of Clays cooked curries to eat when Clay left Wendy Lou's.

And both men knew the Chupacabra was real, why not, Big Foot and Red Bottom Baboons of Alaska were real.

*

"Gee up ugly critters," The Prettiest Thing Created urged her 4x4 on. Since it was a convertible she now and again took a handoff the wheel and cracked a whip from the open roof.

"**Tonka save me,**" Clay in the back where Chelsea Lou had put him to steady the treks, and to ogle him in her mirror OFTEN.

"**Lord save me,**" Sheriff bottom whispered seeing her peeking at Clay and whipping and the 4x4 doing its own thing, bouncing so Nathan now and again popped out the roof seeing the beauty of Texas, prairie dogs scampering, road runners challenging the vehicle and wild mustangs, Comanche warriors forgetting their film set was two miles yonder, not this lot so whopped and let fly rubber arrows, and circling vultures put runny white stuff onto Nathan and any confidence Nathan had left him.

Clay saw Nathan's head appear periodically as he octopus fashion tried vainly to keep the treks down.

"Gee up beauty," Martha beside him on her horse and Clay knew she meant him as she was leering at him, and he started counting how many times a minute those appendages bobbed.

He also wondered how these people stayed alive riding out here.

"Howdy partner," Martha's cowboy, and Clay startled released his hold on the treks and disappeared into the air towards Martha.

"Caught you handsome," she well, it was cooing, and Clay almost wet his pants for on the way over he saw Tonka again and 'Peach and Cherry' those female appendages about to poke his eyes out when landing on Martha.

But his racing heart did not calm down as he lay across her lap, he saw the ground racing close under him, he felt car sick, well horse sick then.

Then all stopped.

"Thank you, Tonka," Clay muttered.

"Rustling Chupacabra, do your job lawman," Martha pulling Clay up by his hair so he could look.

He saw open cleavage not Chupacabra and smiled showing expensive dental worked teeth gleaming white.

Martha allowed him a few seconds peeking, then dumped him.

Clay heard a vehicle door open, and a body dumped beside him.

"These people are rough," Nathan beside Clay having been pushed out to do his JOB.

Holsters and pistols were snow dropped upon them.

The cowhand aboard the four by four joined them with horses' reins, were they insane these folk?

"My boys had blisters all over their sensitive parts, my boys drive police patrol vehicles, not donkeys, giggle."

And as Martha rode into the horizon looking for a war, Chelsea Lou stood behind the lawmen, silent, with X ray eyes borrowed from 'Wonder Woman,' she summoned the men up in one word, 'HAPLESS.'

Clay turned and jumped a foot startled as he had forgot Chelsea Lou and jumping put his arms out knocking the ten-gallon sheriff hat sideways.

"My he is a shrimp," Chelsea Lou looking at the boyish figure of Nathan.

Nathan gave a baby smile, it was deliberate, he was ogling and with a START she realized it and that the boy in front of her was a dwarf, a midget, a small man, but all three made a lecherous MAN.

Nathan knew he had her cooking meals for him, washing his socks, ironing his Y fronts and Giant Panda shaped cod piece.

Chelsea Lou knew otherwise.

Clay not to be out done puffed up his chest and tricks he learned from a man called 'Johnny Christy' in Alaska, undid his shirt buttons showing a dazzling white laundered vest as Clay knew meant Chelsea knew he had on white shorts that every male knew filled a girl with passion.

Chelsea Lou was impressed by the blinding whiteness; he must be washing in Mr. Sparkle.

Clay posed chewing imaginary gum; **he knew he had her cooking meals for him, washing the plates after, flossing his teeth, ironing his 'Yogi Bear'**

shaped cod piece, and cleaning his ears out.

Chelsea Lou knew otherwise.

Then cigar smoke filled their presence and a banjo twanged, then silence broken by a mouth organ.

"Sheriff, I think that cacti is moving," Clay's ogled eyes.

"Where are your colts, Clay?"

Chelsea Lou nodded as the cacti peeled off to reveal a man in a fold down sombrero covered in bandoleros.

Grenades were his male earrings.

"No, go away, we met her first," "*my boys.*"

The man in the sombrero had blue eyes that gave Chelsea Lou his name, phone number, Zip Code and expect me for dinner, hand feed me, wipe my mouth and tuck me into bed with a Tale from Far Away Fairy Land read by you that meant a King-sized bed.

Chelsea Lou knew otherwise.

Then out of the folded down lumpy cacti he emptied out a Chupacabra.

Dead of course, or was it?

A beaver trap was about the critter's neck.

With finger movements the newcomer suggested to "my boys," to dump the creature into the back of the 4x4.

"It is dirty, not going anywhere near my vehicle," Chelsea Lou protested.

Nathan and Clay looked at each other, no way they were carting the Chupacabra back to town, it was twitching.

Mouth organ music filled the air and exhaust smoke, electric green vehicles had not reached this part of Texas.

"He has gone and done it again," Sheriff Nathan feeling just wind in his tummy tonight.

"Johnny Christy, if I was not a pacifist, I did be a

murderer," Clay hoping Terlingua had an all-night 'EATS.'

"Let us laugh, he had not been to Terlingua yet, giggle."

Nathan being smallest held the deflated cacti open while Clay dropped the scratching Chupacabra in by the mangy tail, then spent ten minutes wiping his hands clean rubbing them in the soil.

Clay knew he did be heaving the cacti over a shoulder as Nathan was too small, and together started walking to town.

A warm gentle breeze hit them, yes hit them, coffee was smelt, town was not all that far away.

"Sizzling eggs and Texan refried beans Chili Con Carne Flavor and a flaming hot chili bean dish covered in green stuff the Mexicans like," Nathan allowing his stomach to think and shrink away from third degree burns.

"I wonder what she will cook for me?" Clay slipping up because he meant Chelsea Lou. *"WAR HAD BEEN DECLARED and the two men were no longer BEST OF FRIENDS, again, over a 'skirt, giggle and seeing Fili Pek lingering above the men giving spiritual energy to keep walking, for Clay to dump the cacti on Nathan, and for the two men to forget Chelsea Lou, and be BEST OF PALS AGAIN, fat chance.*

I gave a dog whistle to Fili Pek who looked over at my energy and showed him a hem.

All thoughts of helping the boys ended, he was thinking HEMS, ELASTICS and Earthly passions to keep him trapped as a spirit guide to learn lessons about helping others, and FAT CHANCE, giggle."

"Zing," the first bullet overhead, then dozens of "Zings," as two ranch groups galloped about them, Rodeo King's, and Martha's.

A grenade launcher was fired from horse back and the rear flame singed, well burnt to a crisp a 'DD,' cowboy levelling his automatic reloading pistol at Nathan's head, and luckily, he was singed as the bouncing movement of his horse he did have shot instead, *"my magnificent specimen of manhood, Clay Eagle, then a spirit guide did have broken the heavenly rules and gone rabid, giggle."*

The force of the grenade launcher also threw the man off his horse.

Martha from her cleavage threw out smoke grenades shrinking her bra size.

Her handyman cowboy Kit beside her holding up a two-inch steel shield, where he got that from, no idea, to reflect incoming "ZINGS."

"ZINGS that peppered Nathan's ten-gallon hat, giggle."

ZINGS that flew about Clay's midriff taking the head of his enlarged codpiece, and he *"Tittered, to Nathan as his secret was out how he impressed the likes of Chelsea Lou and Martha to get free meals, washing done, haircuts, massages, fingernails cleaned and toenails cut, even the belly button DE fluffed, and jealousy overcame me, an Earthly rush from the 'Ruler of Earth,' and I was glad, Clay would be all mine soon, titter.*

I glanced over at Fili Pek and yes, the fink was wobbling his torso showing a massive cod piece, so I had to laugh, and Fili Pek came over for a hug.

How could I resist his boyish actions?

It was when his energy started to fumble with the invisible elastics that I knew he was a MAN and threw the BURKE into another dimension.

Do not come back," I hollered."

Anyway.

"I got you bullocks now," Rodeo King screamed and coughed, those smoke grenades Martha was throwing was taking effect.

The boys clung to each other as Rodeo King above them on his horse pointed an assault rifle at them, on automatic so he would not miss and just to lazy to reload.

But it was the Chupacabra returning as a horde of barbarians that saved the boys.

"Gr," "snarl," "snap," "ouch my jewels," "woof," "The horse is bronco loco, help me Rodeo King," and was repeated many times with variations as the badmen looked to their Boss for inspiration.

And got none.

A Chupacabra had jumped onto his lap licking his face, 'Dolly' was on the name tag.

"It was after all related to a dog, giggle."

"God save me," Rodeo King as his horse like a bullet took fright and his men followed, followed by the pack of laughing Chupacabra.

Martha was still, everyone was still, the smoke was so heavy no one could see anything.

Then a ship's foghorn blared, and souls left their bodies.

"Jump in boys, still got the Chupacabra?" Chelsea Lou taking a finger of her vehicle horn.

Texan girls did things big.

Huge men, well-oiled horses, an immigrant side kick who did lay down his life for his mistress, *"Oh Yeh, wonder why?"* Bigger melons than Dolly P., big babies, and bigger filled diapers, yes, Texan girls did it bigger.

Clay Eagle threw an empty cactus into the back and tried to get into the passenger area, but someone had locked the door.

He saw Nathan's fingers pointing to the back and heard the vehicle go into gear and with a running jump Clay landed on the empty cacti suit Johnny Christy had come to town in.

Clay Eagle heard raucous laughter come from the passenger area.

A purple bra was flung against the smoky glass partition.

Then a red stocking.

Frillies.

Ted print 'Y' Fronts

Yogi Bear was giving him a middle finger.

The smell of home cooking.

A vision of a white buffalo came to him, Clay swatted it away, he was hearing war drums.

Clay Eagle was foaming at the mouth.

Flying insects began to stick there as the vehicle sped to town. There were so many Clay began swallowing and eventually choking, Texan bugs are big.

He fell to his knees and held a hand to the glass partition, managing to tap it.

The glass partition opened, "What do want for dinner boy?" Chelsea Lou asked and there was meaning in the word, 'BOY.'

Clay cheered and was amazed Chelsea was clothed.

"She always was, just jealousy had made the deputy **hallucinate** *what he thought about, always, men, think with their bottoms, giggle."*

Character Update Clay Eagle

I knew fame and fortune lay outside the reservation in Alaska. I wanted what I saw in the films, sunny beaches, floozy girls, Marlin Fishing with a camera, and to get it to be a lawman's side kick so answered Nathan's ad.

Here was my chance at fame.

And became a famous cryptid hunter and never taken seriously again.

"He speaks louds of rubbish, do not listen to him," greetings by Time Magazine Reporters.

"He is Tonto's cousin twenty times removed so forget his name, but is some sort of lawman arresting ghosts," and laughter did greet me and saddened me as beautiful people tapped the side of their heads.

"My name is, Tonto's cousin twenty times removed, what am I saying, I am Clay Eagle, famous for arresting Big Foot in Alaska," and was greeted by, "Away you go Nuttery," and thrown out of the Eats Dinner.

[CHAPTER 3] — A GUN FIGHT AT THE TERLINGUA OK CORAL.

Chelsea hit the ship horn multiple times till the whole population of Terlingua came out of their abode houses, wooden cabins, dingy hot hotel rooms, mines, stables, the pub Purple Haze and from cooking barbecued Texan refried beans and ground hogs covered in Paul Newman's special Barbecue Sauce, not to mention a tidy wooden house with pink curtains and windowsill flowerpots.

Whose establishment was this place smalling of perfumes, a sickly-sweet poignant smell, the smell of brass, the smell of leather wallets, and look a sweet girl in a closed pink smoking jacket watering the yellow roses in the flowerpots in the windowsill, and why had she been sleeping all day, what was her line of work, need we ask, yes but since **it is a secret** we are not telling you.

Look is that Texas BIG chickens gobbling bird seed below in the front yard being fed by a sweet innocent girl in another closed pink smoking jacket, and in one hand a basket full of BIG chicken eggs.

In a swirl of dust Chelsea stopped the vehicle sideways on. Outside this strange establishment were laughter cold still be heard coming from the cellars, SELLARS, plural, what a strange establishment, who owned it.

A secret so there.

Chelsea held up a handbrake to wear Nathan had been.

Oh well, end of silly joke and tossed the handbrake in a compartment with other car bits and ends, like a brake pedal.

And several sweet girls in garage overhauls appeared out of that funny smelling house to fix the 4x4.

And Chelsea kissed her fingers and patted their cheeks with those kisses.

"Think our boys might be out of luck here giggle. This girl had Texan refried Cowboy Stew humor giggle, but not as good as mine, ok, better than mine."

The towns people gathered around two places, one group staring at Nathan's rump as his head was buried in the town

High Street dust, where he had landed.

"And the governments paying millions in advertisement to wear a SEAT BELT giggle, idiotic lawman."

And the other group were looking up at Clay Eagle hanging by his hands to a tree that looked like a 'Hanging Tree.'

His belt buckle had also come unhinged contrary to the television advertisements on the item.

Now Chelsea had passed her driving test so could read number plates a distance, she was ogling a Giant Panda cod piece with the front blown off, wondering if her new BOY was now really a boy and no longer a man, *"Oh dear."*

Clay felt his fingers open one by one so he dropped, and the crowd could have made a human hand blanket to catch him.

"THUD."

"Nope, they did not, preferred to hear breaking bones and moans and groans.

"These were the descendants of the Alamo survivors, Judge Roy Bean the Hanging Judge, and those he hung, and since there were no survivors, the descendants of tough wagon train settlers, they wanted more entertainment than what Terlingua offered, A Hot Chili World Contest Yearly, so was a long wait.

They were bored as the ground hogs ate the cable television wiring, so people spent their time ground hog hunting, then barbecuing the rodents in hottest chili, yes, vermin, giant rats living in burrows.

Why hottest chili? This is Texas were all is rememberable.

Terlingua already had the Hot Head Chili Day, they were trying to get a Ground Hog Day, were you dressed up as male or female ground hogs and drank to the extremes, and Line Dancing was all night on High Street.

And 'No Hunting Ground Hog Day the same day as some

drunk seeing all of them folk in ground hog costumes, well, they had a lynching tree in Terlingua.

Anyway, "Boy, better come with me boy," Chelsea and had used 'boy' twice.

"Boy," it began as a whisper and turned into a chant, "BOY,"

"CHELSEA GOT A NEW BOY."

Clay followed Chelsea passing a cemetery with broken crosses and vultures atop them watching him.

He wondered if the last boy fed those overgrown pigeons and heard, "Get the other boy for me please, love you all," Chelsea and Clay heard moans and a body being dragged to where he was.

WAS, yes, through a dusty shaky pink wooden turn turntable door into a palace.

Gold wall papering, native American Cigar statues for hanging whatever onto.

Stuffed bears, mountain lions, beavers, groundhogs, birds, snakes, and the crowd followed in.

A barman in just a white apron appeared, of course he had Y fronts, this is a respectable harmless children's tale of vicious aggravated harm.

"Drinks are not on me," Chelsea said wisely.

The entire adult population of Terlingua stopped moving at those words, but curiosity, a power of the unseen ruler of Earth got the better of them.

They wanted to know about 'BOY,' and the small man they dragged in.

Someone put Line Dancing Music on a machine and in no time the place was full of fifty-eight adults guzzling cold beer with no name.

"Yes, no famous American name as was illegally brewed in

one of the cellars under the floorboards. How many cellars did this establishment have, **not telling**.

Chelsea walked up to the lawmen and threw them dungarees, of course after using a thumb like an artist to get the right body portions on 'BOY.'

What she threw at the small one did not matter, it looked like it belonged to that stuffed battery operated monkey on the bar that hit cymbals, of course when batteries where available.

"The lawmen had no choice, Clay's deputy trousers had been vandalized as he hung above the street, and as Nathan had his head stuck in that street, opportunist children of the same size as him pulled off his sheriff pin stripe 'Wild Bill Hitchcock' trousers and spurs, boots, and light blue penguin print socks. They did leave him his underwear and Yogi Bear cod piece as was taught well by mummy, "Never use public conveniences to do your dump, you will catch S.T.D.

In other words, these lawmen were showing their knees, giggle."

As soon as Nathan put on his orange rag he started scratching.

"What sleeps in here, the cat?" he asked wanting out of them, "where are our donkeys?"

"Yeh, say hello to 'Giggles,' Chelsea threw back indicating with a finger where and what was 'Giggles.'

"Titter," sounds escaped Nathan.

"But that is," Clay stopped his sentence as the mountain lion attracted by his voice eyed him as a delicious raw *Texan pulled pork belly steak.*

"Go welcome our new lawmen come to save us from the Chupacabra ha he ha," Chelsea and to encourage the huge animal threw someone's left over steak bone towards Clay who automatically inched backwards till he was about a meter from the steak.

Giggles the mountain lion, so cute, picked up the steak and flopped on his feet munching away, content in a new friendship.

THEN THEY WERE SAVED, Martha came to town.

So did Rodeo King and the badmen.

And the furless vampire Chupacabra.

"Better put your badge on Sheriff, you will find spares in the jailhouse at the bottom of High Street," Chelsea as the population of Terlingua pushed the lawmen outside in their rush to get best viewing positions of the coming gun fight.

And to take mobile pictures of the Chupacabra and send them viral, and no one would believe the photos thinking it a tourist publicity stunt by the Terlingua City Council.

"Run best friend Nathan," Clay advising picking up Nathan as he was so small and explains why women found him so cuddly, why in his one piece 'Yogi Bear,' pajamas they could tuck Nathan under an arm pit and feel secure, and dream of 'Yellowstone National Park," and all the souvenirs they could buy.

Deputy Clay had no idea where he was running, except at the end of the street called, 'High,' was the jailhouse and if unlocked, he could shut the escaped asylum inhabitants out.

"What 'High Street?" He asked.

"*Rattle,*" his native American guide being ever so helpful.

It was the glint of silver on a badge that pulled Clay to the left between two tepees and there was this adobe building with an ever so 'Rollie Polly' man standing outside watching them.

He must have been 60 stone.

"Hey sheriff, we are lawmen, help," but Clay never finished his sentence as disappointment filled him as he reached the door the large man had vanished inside the jailhouse slapping and locking the door with a loud sliding click.

Clay put down Nathan who stood and dusted himself and threw away his flea infested rag onto a badman riding close by.

Wrapped about his face so the bad man fell off with a thud and lay motionless seeing stars and stripes and fleas in front of him.

"I knew you had True Grit," Martha liking what she had seen thinking it a deliberate act, **but we know better.**

Perhaps there was more to Sheriff Nathan Bottom, and he intended that violence, taking out his stress on an innocent passing cowboy about to blow his head off, well, **it will be our secret then.**

Next that mountain lion fearful for a new friend danced over the heads of badmen to land heavily on Clay's feet so explains why he pulled funny faces.

"I really like this, the stuff of a marvel Comic," Martha blazing away at the retreating bad men with a 40-caliber heavy machine gun self-assembled from her deep cleavage, so in an instant our two lawmen and a big Cat were covered in bronze spent shells.

And the smell of cordite.

"Yippee Yahoo," it was a foolish act of bravado, but Rodeo King had to save face as his band of merry men in their emblazoned chaps waited a distance from him, with bad thoughts of replacing him as they were bad men who of course had bad thoughts, it went with the job.

Rodeo King rode right up to our boys with automatic pistols firing away at our lawmen and because a moving horse is moving, he missed them and shot away the jail door hinges of the jailhouse front door that creakily swung open.

There stood the other sheriff eating from a box of chocolate doughnuts, behind him piles of empty doughnut boxes with insects running free to eat the sugary crumbs.

Wiping his sweet icing fingers across his dropping red moustache and light blue jeans he said, **it might be a secret on his part** as he should not try speaking and swallowing at the same time so went BLUE.

"Never mind Martha threw in our boys and faced this man with a protruding belly, giggle."

"Neigh," Martha's horse inside the jail violently swiping a tail across this sheriff, then did stuff horses reserve for outside. This horse obviously did not like this man and remembered past grievances and *was a revengeful horse, mean when it wanted.*

"Neigh," the animal "neighed," it was laughing.

"C**p," the sheriff running to the back of the jailhouse and out a handy back door.

"Rodeo King will avenge me," thus proving the horse right.

"I am not working in this latrine Nathan," Clay Eagle gasping for air avoiding the **horse action end** just in case.

"Deputy, go get a mop," Sheriff Nathan looking up at Martha hoping to see promises in her stare showing her who was top lawman here so deserved the free *Texan Crockpot Sweet Spicey Brisket Sandwich Ground Hogs.*

Yes, she stared down at him, "My, you are small?" She said backing her horse out the front door.

"Neigh," the horse and then licked Nathan and Clay with a rough tongue.

"Aw, the horse likes you," Martha and, "be back with grub boys."

That vitalized Clay into mopping and Nathan found

cowboy clothes for them both, soap and towel, a kettle for hot water and some perfumed aftershave and being such good friends Nathan did not use it all up on himself, he left a drop for Clay who was smelling of antiseptic floor mop water.

Martha was sure to be attracted by the lavender essence coming from Nathan.

"Yes, they were the best of friends, giggle."

"Howdy boys," Chelsea just walking in, well there was no doorbell, and the door was still open, horse manure takes a while to vacate, but Texans are used to the smell as they are Texans, and a true Texan has a horse not a trek bike.

Chelsea put down a big cake box and the smell from it was not cake but Texan Refried Chili Beans, extra chili, and Austin-Style Megas with Black Beans.

What is Migas, stale bread, scrambled eggs with tortilla strips, black beans and why not just call it scrambled eggs, why because this is The Lone Star State.

Then Martha came in and pushed Rodeo King ahead of her, her cowboy friend Kit having a gun in his groin, and that made Rodeo King tame and allowed himself to be locked up in the single cell out back, yes out back, out the handy back door the other sheriff had went through and there it was, an adobe igloo with a heavy wooden door with a padlock.

No windows must be sweltering in there, as it was an old Native American sweat house to cleanse the soul for meditation, an antique crawling with big Texan biting insects.

Never mind, the law was not that cruel, there was a hole in the roof for the smoke to escape, but there was no more fire lighting these days, so the hole allowed flies and those big biting insects in.

"Poor Rodeo King, giggle."

"He will not be here long, we will all get drunk tonight and lynch him," the cowhand Kit.

"Excuse me, who are you?" Nathan asked as he was smart, he needed these people, especially Martha so was not saying, "We are the law, no lynching's here."

"He is Kit," Martha popped up allowing her men to come in and dump *Texan Crockpot Sweet Spicey Brisket Sandwich Ground Hogs*, food on the sheriff desk.

"I heard 'Rot Gut,' being drank, yes, Chelsea always a businesswoman was selling stuff she made from corn in her cellar, "a lynching tonight," she shouted in the direction where Rodeo King was.

"I am the sheriff here, no lynching Martha, Chelsea, sorry, and what is he getting hung for?" Nathan asked.

"Breeding Chupacabra," Martha throwing an armpit over Nathan's head as she looked down at him scratching fast the top of his head, so the friction caused it to smoke.

"Hey," Nathan alarmed as Kit buckled six shooters on his waist.

"I got my Colts Nathan," Clay spinning his shooters and Chelsea smiled. He was now letting Chelsea handle them, showing her the silver work so their hands tangled.

"I was so jealous, here Fili Pek you about. And Fili Pek appeared so I kicked him in the groin as was jealous of Chelsea, and why do that to Fili Pek, he was handy."

Then mouth organ music filtered down from the roof.

"Better get the cavalry as the badmen will come free Rodeo King," Johnny Christy in a deep put on Southern accent.

The girls attracted by the music like the rats of Hamelin went outside to look for the source.

Cigar smoke drifted down and a red-hot cigar butt twirled somehow from the roof into the jailhouse.

It landed on the top of Nathan's head.

"Jesus Christ, I am on fire, help me Clay," Nathan and

Clay emptied the nearest water container he saw, the spittoon that needed emptying last year.

The boys were left in the jailhouse, the folk all gone, the girls away with Johnny Christy for somehow he had got off the roof onto a horse and moved out to a campfire, Johnny's camp site where *Texas Chicken Fried Steaks with sizzling Gravy* was waiting for the girls just like that at the click of a finger, and how did Johnny Christy manage that, remember from Alaska it was revealed he was a secret federal agent, the best as he kept **his secrets to himself so there.**

"Well Nathan, I am hungry."

"After we eat, we put on our tin stars and show this place the law is here," Nathan.

"And the boys ate *Texan Crockpot Sweet Spicey Brisket Sandwich Ground Hogs,* prairie rats for short, fluffy fat looking gophers but still rodents, rats without tails,

and the extra chili was extra hot to hide the fact the boys were eating RAT.

"I am on fire again," Nathan.

"So am I," Clay.

Post Script. And just how did Johnny manage to get onto the jailhouse roof and away with the two women in less than thirty seconds?

Only Johnny knows sorry.

Character Update Johnny Christy.

Johnny watched the F.B.I. Files as a child, Remakes of Elliot Ness, James Bond 007 Films, The British Queens Xmas Message, and his Presidents Tooth fairy Message and knew when he grew up has to be 008 and have gold painted floozy girls flamingo dance for him, clean out his private swimming pool while dancing, the toilet on his private jest while dancing, the boilers in his private steam yacht while dancing, yes he was to be 008 **and a secret.**

And first met the boys Nathan and Clay in Alaska chasing the Big Foot and stealing the limelight from our hapless boys, and the girls Madam Wendy Lou and Cindy Lou.

And now he was in Texas with the girls in a big RV Texan style, and an immigrant Big Foot looking for the sun on the RV roof in dark sunglasses and under that a cut out face of a man who was once Mr. Universe.

Johnny knew where the boys went so did publicity, the boys got the trashy parts and he the glory, and the new girls the boys were kind enough to introduce him to.

"Is the desire to have gold painted dancing girls attend me that drives me," Johnny Christy truthfully.

I learned mouth organ and banjo as realized girls swoon over one and line dance over the other.

I get all my house chores down from the girls I steal from those idiots so am pushed forward to collect girls to my aviary, that way they can have days off and feed me grapes as I lounge strumming a toy harp singing my poetry.

See a clean tale with nothing happening between the sheets that I know off.

"OH, sweety when are you coming back to the hammock," a sweet voice, was that Madam Wendy Lou and shows Johnny Christy speaks a load of RUBBISH.

I have two right now, Madam Wendy Lou and Cindy Lou and see the boys think they are going to be fed *Texan Chicken Chalupas*, those cheesy tangy tortilla pasties by them girls Marth and Chelsea, but I need more love to be the best secret federal agent ever, and I am hungry.

I have drawn up a thirty-course menu, "Here apes jump down from the R.V. roof and give this to Cindy Lou as I cannot hear pots and pans and smell the heat of an oven, a single peanut in nit, good ape," Johnny as the ape went inside.

"What does that bas***d take us girls for," Cindy Lou.

"I heard that," Johnny and blew cigar rings through the kitchen window.

Silence except for the sound of pots and pans and rubber chickens prepared for dinner.

Like the girls said, "What does that bas***d take us girls for?"

And Johnny played his mouth organ and soon he heard contented sighs from the hot oven of the R.V.

"Works every time," as he played his soothing mouth organ.

An ape lay on the roof of the R.V. with starry eyes wanting his autograph.

He was Johnny Christy, not 008 but 001 and would enjoy his tenderized rubber chicken.

And in case he got bunged, the girls had put in a laxative.

They were girls that is why.

CHAPTER 4 ESCAPE

Chupacabra a cross between something?

"Yippee Yahoo," the badmen hollered riding horses that stopped dead at the far end of High Street, rearing so the badmen could wave their cowboy hats in the air, then ride again firing six shooters at anything that moved so missed everything as anything that moved had stopped moving and hid.

And by the time they got to the Jailhouse the soil rocked with the sound of horse's hooves, and they needed to reload.

Not so Martha and her men who saw the chance to lasso these badmen and have lynching's tonight.

And they were boozy as Chelsea Loo was a good businesswoman.

Ever see these John Wayne cowboy films, yes there must be a fist fight were not a black eye appears, bust lips or toothless grin, bleeding head from a bottle bash, men stumbling holding kicked in cod pieces, stretcher bearers sneaking others to the doctors with bust bones, well this was not one of those films.

"Glad we are being sensible Nathan," Clay stroking his new friend the mountain lion.

And as a bra tangled Nathan's neck who replied, "Are you seeing what I am seeing Clay?"

"Sure, am friend."

"Purr."

Now because the boys were peering into the dust to identify who was braless, a rollie poli sheriff drew up at the back of the jailhouse.

"Rodeo King come," he shouted but no one heard him because of the din so he dismounted the children's pony and went to Rodeo King who in handcuffs was peering into the dust cloud as another bra had sailed onto Clay, it was PURPLE and Clay remembered his time in the back of the 4x4.

And wondered if Nathan had the time and BRAINS to learn any Johnny Christie tricks?

"Best friends still giggle? Of course?"

It was a huffing puffing overweight sheriff who staggered to the other children's pony with Rodeo King who was still in a state of surprise at being startled, or was he?

"That was not a horse he was being led too; it was something escaped from a petting zoo, giggle."

Then a "ZING," passed under his legs slicing open a ventilation opening in those hot tight denim jeans that bulged places as Texans liked to show they were bigger than you.

So, in a Nano second Rodeo King was on that pony using his feet on the dust to help the animal go faster out of town.

Behind him ran a huffing puffing rollie poly sheriff whose pony had had enough carrying him and vamoosed after the other pony.

The ponies were best friends.

Then the Chupacabra pack ran amok in that dust cloud of fist fighting men snapping and salivating over friend and foe.

Now it is said some Chupacabra look like skinny old men, with big glass ogling eyes and the spines running down the back, that common Chupacabra trait. These ones had webbed fingers capable of stealing your wallet, snatching your Texan Hash of your plate, pulling your braces, and letting go, of ogling the girls at Chelsea's behind those pink curtains and the Purple Haze, because they were skinny old male Chupacabra whatever, *"looking for a leg to hump, a male is a male and proves males evolved from worms, algae found in drainage sites, English Mustard and were not divinely created, giggle."*

Did that mean the other Chupacabra when they got elderly became these types with fingers capable of stealing your false teeth out of your mouth?

Of using your stolen credit cards at the A.T.M.

They were Chupacabra and let men think they were the masters and had them trained, *"just let the men think, the Chupacabra just knew where free food was for doing 'Play dead tricks.'*

Now the fighting stopped, the dust settled, and men said, "Devil dogs are here, lawmen do your job."

"Yes, do your job and stop ogling," I shouted but was ignored.

And Clay was next to Chelsea Lou holding his shirt over her front to the annoyance of the good, bad, and ugly cowboys with broken limbs, black eyes, toothless grins, and bleeding heads.

Nathan held up an orange towel picked up in front of Martha who did not recognize it, but a friendly mountain lion did and sprang just like that. Men thought Martha was cat food and one cowboy who loved her in slow motion sprang towards the big cat.

And the big cat only wanted its orange sleeping rag back and took it and ran off towards Chelsea's bar and home.

And that lonesome cowboy sailed by Martha and was too close for comfort, so Martha went berserk.

And his name was Kit and the same who rode with her earlier, he was her handsome know all about cow's foreman.

"We got a lynching boy," and the drunken fools, see Chelsea had trained her bargirls, had been selling her moonshine to all so all were drunk except our sensible boys.

"Martha, I love you," the cowhand Kit.

"Sorry Kit, you got to close as felt your unshaven whiskers, smelt the beans, Texan Cajun Cake, smelt the farts the beans made still clinging to you, smelt the stale tobacco breathe, smelt the moonshine on you, and smelt the prairie on you, you stink, never come close to me again," Martha was annoyed **and a woman's excuse.**

"Well, what are you going to do about this lynching sheriff?" Chelsea asked from the window of her 4x4.

Nathan peered, yes, he was sure that was Clay in the passenger seat.

Clay pretended not to see his ex-best friend.

"Et Tu Brutus," Nathan pulling on his borrowed trousers and seeing a sleeping cat trod on the tail to ruin the romantic atmosphere and out of jealous meanness.

A horrific shriek filled the air and folk covered their ears and stopped the lynching to see who had stopped the fun.

"Sorry boys, I am the law here, let the man go," it just took one brave fool.

"We never had the law before," another one.

"Better off without them," another.

"He is so small it will be easy to lynch him as well," a third.

"But this was the shrimp who had high kicked Rodeo King, the

shrimp was a martial artist and painted good landscapes, giggle, but there were just too many oh dear cannot look but am giggle."

A passenger door on a 4x4 opened and a handsome Native American went to meet Tonka as he flew into the fray with these words, "Best friend Clay is here."

What a fight, men with toothless grins, broken bones, bashed bleeding heads and braless women got the better of both lawmen.

So, what saved our heroes?

A heavy caliber machine gun fired into the air from the back of a 4x4.

"The lawmen are paying a round at mine boys and girls," Chelsea who was a good businesswoman.

"We split the bill Nathan," Clay worried he would not be able to take Chelsea out to the local diner for Ground Hog Burgers covered in a Newman sauce to go with tailless rodents.

"Phish', we will get the town council to pay Clay so relax friend," Nathan confident.

And the town council heard and laughed sitting in the driver's seat in a 4x4.

But it was a woman who saved the men.

And the crowd cleared leaving our lawmen standing sitting does not matter, what does is that they were surrounded by thirsty Chupacabra more interested in water than BLOOD, except a few older ones, reptilian scaly critters whose fingers were counting dollars in stolen wallets and throwing away credit cards, as knew not the pin or the human to extract the pin from by threatening to hump a leg lizard style.

And a whistle blew and was faint as come from afar summoning the Chupacabra to the whistle blower, and the silly animals went instead of heading into Mexico, freedom, party time and meals for they were loaded with stolen cash they did give the whistle blower to party in Mexico.

"Think we better forget meals tonight, Clay," Sheriff Bottom and was a lie, he was wanting Clay to yawn and go to bed so he could go for Refried Texas Roadhouse Chili Beans with Chelsea Loo by sneaking out the handy jailhouse back door.

"Yawn, all this yahoo has made me tired Nathan my best friend," *"the lying creep Clay giggle. Yes, Clay did sneak out the handy back door of the jailhouse and head for Chelsea Lou's, the bedding in the jailhouse was two single straw stuffed mattresses. He knew by experience a woman's mattress was soft, imported from a fine furniture store.*

And as Terlingua became broke because of a smart businesswoman Chelsea who never gave away a free drink, someone paid.

Now Martha cleaned herself up at her Silver Dollar spread, and what a spread to keep her cow hands LOYAL.

Well of course there was her imported Transylvanian Castle full of mod coms, a flushable toilet, a walk-in shower, great just strip off casting dusty stuff across the house to the shower, and was of course deliberate, for all her incarnations against Kit she had laid a trail.

Martha was a secret woman, a secret to herself.

*"All that demeaning of Kit her trusted foreman **was show**, and he put up with her frolics as long as they did not turn serious and put him out of his managerial job of bossing people, he had watched remakes of 'Raw Hide,' and wore silver spurs, all the cowboy gear so was weighted down and beginning to get a curved back and be bowed legged from horse riding and they say if you ride a horse to long, you become impotent, maybe why the ancient Scythians died out and Martha knew her classics?*

So, Clay headed for the goal and a bunk bed with the lights off, he was pretending to go to bed so did not want Nathan to see him quickly exit out the handy back door and head for Chelsea's.

And Nathan pushed the jailhouse door shut and turned off the light in his room, a room that served as reception, cooking area, latrine and sleeping quarters on an army fold down cot, big size for the other departed sheriff.

"Was it Robert Burns who said something like, "The best laid plans of mice and men often go astray? Giggle."

It happened thus.

"With all that celebrating sounds from Chelsea's I need to tip toe across High Street to her house and tell her I need a shower and latrine as the jailhouse has only a big bucket for multiple uses," Nathan showing he was quick thinking and on the ball.

"With all the shouting coming from Chelsea's and the Purple Haze I can find my way to Chelsea's in this pitch-dark night, Oh Tonka which sounds are from Chelsea's, do I turn right or left," Clay who as a newcomer to town had no idea where to go and Chelsea being a good businesswoman and town council did not provide street lighting.

And in the Purple Haze an overweight sheriff wanted back to the jailhouse to retrieve his collection of certain types of magazines, "There is no loo paper in that jailhouse so why I keep a collection of magazines in angel cake boxes."

"Do you hear him, and he expects you to believe that tripe? Giggle."

And Giggles a mountain lion was lonely for its new friends so had raided the kitchen of Chelsea's and helped herself to half a carcass of lamb to share with a new friend. It was a mighty strong animal and a thieving beast.

"We not going to take this lying down are we Rodeo

King?" Jesse asked acting brave knowing they were not going back to town so he could talk BIG.

"I want you to go back to town Jesse and see what the lawmen are up to, eves drop, then come back here and tell me Jesse, and I will be proud of you," Rodeo King giving Jesse a prep talk knowing he was expendable and not a best friend.

And the pack of Chupacabra were hungry and needed fed but Rodeo King was planning how to get rid of the lawmen so was too busy to attend these monsters needs.

*

"Well Kit, go collect the lawmen and take them back here. They can sleep in the spare adobe house where we keep the sacks of horse grain," she lied to Kit so not to make him murderously jealous for she was to put them in the guest rooms, and there where many for she had built her ranch house after a castle.

It was BIG.

It was called 'Martha's folly.'

It featured once on the front page of Home Beautiful.

On Time Magazine.

She got into Forbes richest list.

Some said guests still roamed the place moaning, "Where is the exit?"

And Mr. Kit was bad, the grain sacks for the horses brought rats and they rattlers and he dreamed of locking the door to that adobe house with our boys in there and dropping the key in what horses leave behind after a meal, no fool not a Nacho Dip, horses do not know how to make that, they do the natural stuff, well, never mind, neigh.

And the scene was set, the actors prepared, no, Chelsea had left the bar to powder her arm pits, brush her teeth, sprinkle talc down her midriff, dribble expensive perfume onto her opened cleavage, and just like that changed her knickers.

No one goes on a date with unchanged smellies, and a shower after today's activities would have been quicker and cleaner, but she was a Texan and was chewing jerky, Tonka flavored to sweeten her breath for her native American Boy.

And spread on her soft mattress, primary school readers for Nathan to read to her a for she had no time to read herself, she was a Texan girl, who had learnt to use a Heavy machine gun, lasso for lynching rustlers, how to make moonshine and to sell the poison, and become a businesswoman with dollars buried out back under the privacy as no one in their right mind did bury cash under a privy, "Gad the pongs," but she was a businesswoman and knew her money was safe there.

Besides the mountain lion guarded her place or was supposed to but a handsome Native American had come to town.

And all had made plans and not read Robert Burns.

It all happens in next chapter to give you time for a quick brew and biscuit.

Character Update Martha

Martha was a Texan woman so had to have big appendages.

A cowgirl who went to a Texan finishing school for girls, the Houston Chicken School so learned all about money that she liked.

It bought things, more cows for one, hired more bow-legged cowboys to look after her cows, and cows meant money to build her castle and be featured as a Presidential Candidate for the Texan Party.

She paid well, her bunk houses were clean and bed bug free, so men queued to work for Martha.

Yet she was lonely, she was unmarried and kept Granny Nanny to make her a warm toddy nights and tuck Martha into bed and Martha was 31.

For a Texan girl she had no Texan boyfriend, so we think, there were bunk houses full of sweaty cowhands, the whole of Texas drooled at her feet so why was she so lonely for love?

"Granny Nanny keeps the nasty men away that is why. Granny Nanny is here for life not to be tossed aside into a retirement home, yes just let some handsome sweaty cowhand try getting past me at night to sneak into Martha's bedroom to tell her saucy action-packed cowhand tales of the west, Granny Nanny knows how to stop them," Granny Nanny opening her room where bear traps, beaver traps, man traps, every shooter imaginable and in the center, a **big** picture of herself.

CHAPTER 5   HIGH MOON

"Squelch," each time Nathan put a sneaky foot down on High Street.

"Judas will the Town Council not pay for a horse s**t sweeper?"

And the town council was peeking out an upstairs boudoir window smelling of expensive perfume that should have paid for a horse s**t sweeper as being a female, knew when sneaky footfalls were a coming her way.

"Mm, where is Clay," a little disappointed at who she saw jumping from pile of manure to pile of manure. "Not coming up the fire escape with those boots on," she added and closed her window, Nathan was disturbing the sleeping essences that now angrily buzzed into the night air and towards a light bulb.

Chelsea switched on the air conditioner, then off, she needs the room extra Texan hot to make her man either take clothes of or prove Instant Combustion happens in humans.

It was also an excuse to change into a what girls wear to go to bed not to sleep but to arouse a boyfriend.

"And noticed Fili Pek was missing and yes there was the perverted spirit guide, clinging to the light bulb fir energy, well he wanted to ogle, he was for it, so excuse me while I close down the portal so you will not hear from me for a while, or hear Fili Pek, giggle."

And Clay headed the wrong way towards the Purple Haze and all the bad, men wanting to put him in a shallow grave and there was only Rattle to save him, "Rattle where are you? Giggle."

"Help," Fili Pek asking for prayers of deliverance from me.

And coming Clay's way a ten-foot rattler out for a night-time snack, gophers that plagued the town as fed well on what ate what the horses dropped, see Chelsea did not need to pay our wages for a horse s**t sweeper when the gophers ate the cleaners that ate that manure.

And her hired staff trapped the gophers and sold them to hungry drinkers in her establishment, 'Chelsea', barbecued parries ground hogs covered in a Newman Texan Chili sauce, extra hot so the eaters did buy more chilled XXX for s throat aflame.

Chelsea was some businesswoman.

And if you were one of her clients you did think it a bargain a barbecued ground hog, two for the price of one because you were seeing double and about to be thrown out the swing doors, flat on the face, or hanging on a horse stand, or in the horse trough, or in that other stuff lying about Nathan had failed to avoid.

And the gopher was either sold onto another person seeing three gophers or taken out the swing doors with the evicted.

Never mind, Chelsea knew things out there ate the barbecued gophers and left the evicted alone, the unknown eaters did not like the smell of BOOZE.

And a large ex-sheriff was tip toing towards the back of the jailhouse, intent on MURDER, he wanted his job Back.

In a hand a bag full of female Chupacabra pee to throw into the jailhouse.

That stink did bring them devil dogs in and hopefully chew the lawmen to nibble sized chunks.

"He ha ho," the evil ex-sheriff and his extended tummy bobbed, and he gasped for breath from the exertion dropping the bag onto his worn out faded needing polished cowboy boots whose heels had worn away.

"Gasp oxygen someone," and was not alone, "what have I done?" Was a fair question.

Firstly, Clay heard him and stopped with these words, "Tonka has let off, gasp oxygen someone."

And a cute mountain lion was just behind Clay with their dinner and stopped dropping the lamb carcass and fainted with a loud, "MEOW."

And lot movement in the shadows alerted the bad sheriff the devil dogs were coming for his boots.

"Got to get them off," he gasped staggering about trying to pull off his worn-out boots that exposed holes in the soles, and added, "oxygen someone," and the shadows became red hot eyes staring at him.

"Tonka forgive me, it is those devil dogs coming here, what do I do Tonka, run for fresh air or save that man who seems drunk ahead," Clay and what do you think he did?

It is a secret for a few paragraphs.

Now Jesse rode into town and dismounted.

"I will make you proud of me Rodeo King and will draw you a map and put X and Y and stick figures here and there as I never learned to read or write," an idiot for "Rodeo King never learned to read or write either so will stare blankly at your art work, then beat the c**p out of you in front of the bad men jeering as was a nights entertainment and took their minds of plotting to assassinate Rodeo King who behind his back gave fingers, of course when Jesse was looking elsewhere or shining Rodeo King's boots or saddle up.

"He was an aspiring creep giggle."

And a Native American guide called, Snake rattle was luring a ten-foot rattle snake away from Clay towards a man standing under a wooden house's verandah drawing sticks.

"Should not you be luring it away with your rattles into the bush Rattle?" And guessed this spirit wanted revenge against Davy Crocket and other Indian Fighters, oh dear what had heaven sent Clay as a guide? Giggle."

And Nathan looked up and saw his angel, Chelsea Lou framed in a window frame, and somehow, she was stuffed in a flesh-colored teddy suit. A small electric fan behind her was on to stop perspiration under the arms and between the legs so her long untied hair fluttered out towards the window glass.

Nathan had a cardiac arrest looking at her and not looking where he was going because he was ogling slipped on slippery stuff, yodeled a bit as he flipped into the air and thudded down on his back with a loud splat.

He released a great stink that wafted towards that angel in a window frame.

"Not tonight cowboy," the angel closing curtains and putting away her collection of 'Learn to read with Noddy and Big Ears.'

"No," Nathan let loose and staggered on, a man with determination and true grit and fell into the horse trough and was cleaned some, and some poor horse would drink from that trough.

Chelsea listened to the drowning sounds under her

window and peeked.

How kind, she threw a bar of perfumed soap down hitting Nathan on the crown.

"Gad that hurt," he cussed rubbing his head then scrub a dub he went in a frenzy to get smelling clean.

And Jesse drew a bath with a star in it and music notes drifting from it for Nathan was happy, he was in love.

And his friend Clay, although fit staggered under the weight of the bad sheriff who had spent a lifetime eating dough nuts. A roll of tummy fell across his eyes blinding him.

In front of him an unconscious cat he was going to miss standing on, was he?

Clay heard the Chupacabra slurping and giggling getting closer.

Those smelly boots were still on the bad sheriff who was enjoying the ride on the back of a handsome native American.

"He was gay, well I never, giggle."

"MEOW," very loud as Clay stood on the 400lb mountain lion.

It saved their lives as the Chupacabra froze with hate, that was one of them big cats that ate them when they were having an afternoon nap with a stomach full of blood sucked from rustled cow or sheep.

The Chupacabra were vampires.

Now we do not know how big cats think, but this one knew Clay was not being shared with them devil dogs, so just like that what was up under Clay and running towards the High Street.

And a smoke bomb sailed through the air and exploded in front of those nasty dogs.

Mouth organ music filled the air.

The smell of freshly caught salmon filled the air.

The big cat ran up a ladder from nowhere to the top of a wooden roof.

"You stink, get away from me," Johnny Christie shoving Clay off the front of the roof and there was a splash.

"Nathan you out and about to, I was looking for an eats as was hungry," Clay fibbing and looked up and there was an angel looking at him, she was spraying lavender air freshener towards him.

"Me also, was so hungry sneaked out so as not to wake you Clay," what a liar Nathan was and looked up and screamed as lavender air freshener got into his eyes, Clays too.

So never saw Johnny Christy go to the end of the roof and push off the overweight sheriff. Do not worry, Johnny knew the bad man did bounce and he bounced onto Jesse.

"Argh," Jesse moaned passing out from lack of oxygen and the smell coming from those boots.

And a passing rattle snake bit both men on their bums to the delight of rattling Snake, Clay's guide. Lucky for them the snake did not inject any venom, it was saving that stuff for rodents up ahead or did go hungry tonight.

Rattling Snake was in a world of his own so ignored the fat the settlers were not dead as he and the snake went into the dark bush.

"There is no doctor in town, get down there and suck the poison out," Jesse told the sheriff who did, and Jesse got more than he bargained for.

"Giggle."

And that is when Kit rode in.

"Well, I never," and everyone has a mobile phone with a camera.

"It is not what it looks like, a rattler bit my bum," Jesse sobbed.

"And bit mine," the sheriff.

"I have heard some lame tales," Kit and turned his horse to gallop away before a bullet took him out.

"Aw no," Jesse not believing his luck as the horse lifted a tail and well, it knew all about Jesse, he fired BANG BANGS at your back so needed blinded.

"I am off," the bad sheriff and headed for Chelsea's.

Would he get in?

"I am riding out of this hell hole," Jesse pulled up his jeans and mounted.

"Oh, my sore bum," he complained as his horse knew the way home, allowing Jesse to sooth his bit bum.

And was bit and covered in other type of bites because the bad sheriff was gay and knew he was dead from the rattler bite as he was in heaven sucking snake bite out of Jesse.

And the Chupacabra tore up his boots, so he walked bare foot towards Chelsea's.

He soon was squelching as stray dogs, horses and cows passed through Terlingua on the way to the river as gets hot under a BIG Texan sun, not to mention what pet cats and that mountain lion left and those marauding Chupacabra. And would Chelsea's staff let him in?

He needs a change of clothes, boots, and a bath in the river as the jailhouse did not have one so this man had a deodorant need.

And mouth organ music and a banjo played from behind Chelsea's curtains.

"How does he do it Nathan?" Clay asked knowing both men did be rummaging the jailhouse for tinned food and a tin opener.

"I got to learn to play a guitar, hear the women like that," Nathan getting out of the trough.

"Yep, and I could sing and shake the pelvis, I hear women like that," Clay out of the trough lifting Nathan out as the trough came up to his shoulders, he was only a small man.

"Well, howdy boys, bathing out Northern fashion," Kit letting the lawmen know he was from Texas and told them Martha was inviting them back for eats.

"How sweet, the boys did be fed, maybe after Martha burned their clothes. And Kit had brought their own horses for them to learn to ride.

AND: "Rodeo King this is all I got to draw and told you why, just look at my bum as is proof a snake bit me," Jesse who quick as a rattler strike, dropped his jeans and paraded his moon.

The bad men looking laughed and made sissy kisses towards Jesse.

"Your moon is covered in kisses Jesse, I swear come six inches near me and I will shoot you dead," Rodeo King and that is why Rodeo King did not beat the c**p out of Jesse that night.

Alone Jesse sat down to think, did he still love Rodeo King and why was he loving him, was he? And wanted to shoot himself for perish the question that will **remain his secret.**

Character Update Chelsea

"I always knew I was beautiful," her and that explains it all.

"I was born in Terlingua so there was not much opposition to being adored apart from her, the cattle rancher, cowgirl with melons glued to her chest," another quote of Chelsea's.

Where were these quotes taken from?

The Brewers Association Magazine of America and Dependencies that is were.

"I sell lots of XXX, pose for the cameras and make sure I

get onto the front pages of anything printed. It is easy; I do not even need to flash my shaven legs but wiggle a cardboard cutout of a leg insured for a million dollars.

In the dim light the cameras think the leg real, especially when my girls dressed as cuddly gophers serve them legal XXX.

Then bill them for nothing in life is free," another quote of hers that was not taken from the Texas Biblical News but the Texas Economist.

She was a businesswoman on the make, much worse than a Scot on the make.

"Run," was the advice given by the local pastor if there was still one, before she opens the 4x4 driver's door and slides a bare leg out.

A leg that will walk to Chelsea's and you will follow the leg, "Run," the local pastor advised.

What happened to him?

Chelsea began to attend church and made sure her legs showed as well as what Martha prized.

"Run," the pastor said and did seeking repentance in a Pastor Rehabilitation Home in Dallas for he had seen, liked, drooled, and lusted over legs.

And now our boys were in Terlingua, would they tame this Jezebel, and would you call a Scotsman on the make Mr. Jezebel for wanting to be rich, richer, much richer, and more loaded rich?

No, "It is because I am a woman and have made men feel inferior, well they are, we all know men evolved Emperor Penguins with a bit of Bull Elephant mixed in to make them feel 'Oh La,' fit for nothing but to buy my illegal XXX, postcards of my girls baking Pecan Pie, the back of me in a bath with a shower hat on and was bought because was supposed to be me, yes men are evolved from the 'Walking Dead' thingmabobs, brainless.

"No, it would take another to tame this shrew, and he plays a mouth organ or did the shrew tame him? Giggle."

CHAPTER 6 MARTHA'S

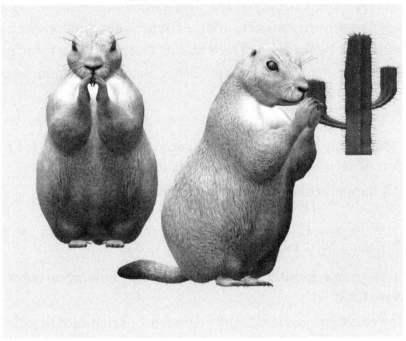

"The trail is hot; it will be easy to follow all that muck back to their nest and eradicate them. If you need help, phone me on the mobile, 50c per minute," Martha had been explaining she would provide camping gear and pack mules for them to go and be lawmen, statues would be erected to the boys ends of High Street, they did have flowers placed at the bottom of each on **Remembrance Sunday.**

It was obvious Martha was not joining the boys on their Texan road trip, she still had on her fluffy cowgirl red slippers.

A faint cigar essence clung to her best cowhide pink dyed

dressing gown.

Martha to annoy the boys or a future promise to the survivor, 'can join me eating refried beans upstairs watching John Wayne western classics,' took of her twenty-gallon Stetson and shook her masses of hair about. The boys were transfixed for as she shook her curls free other appendages bounced out purposely.

For a moment's silence she allowed the boys to ogle.

Now they did go get the devil dogs and Rodeo King for her, after all that is what she paid taxes for.

A banjo strummed summoning her.

With a twirl of blinding light from silver spurs on her fluffy cowgirl boots she was gone.

Nathan's mouth was sagging open allowing a cuprous saliva flow.

Clay could have sworn Tonka came out of that blinding light, and get what Tonka was doing? It was chasing a girl called Tonka.

Clay outstretched a hand and closed Nathan's mouth.

He wiped off saliva into something furry.

Clay escaped having his hand bitten off, his unwanted pet saw its future in that light, it was a ferocious predator not a lap cat, an eater of elks, beavers, antelopes, and men, like these two the God of mountain lions had given her for breakfast.

And as the light vanished so did the urge to eat the boys.

Lucky fellas.

Clay wanted back to Alaska, these people were insane, they obviously knew where the Chupacabra nested and the rustlers, so why had they sent for them to clear them out.

As if reading his thoughts Nathan replied, "We saw that

film, what was it called, 'The Expendables,' yes Clay," Nathan releasing why they had been sent for, they been had.

"It costs money to train a real cow hand, why all the young folk hereabouts run off to the city for exciting jobs in takeaways, car washes, college courses, sex and drugs," Martha understanding the concerns, "why you two took out Big Foot and that monster is a lot bigger than a Chupacabra, a small dog boy."

Clay looked at Martha smiling at him, **where had she come from**, she had vanished with the light and back while they blinked.

"A woman is allowed girlie secrets boys," and blew fresh cigar smoke in rings that encircled the boy's necks like Hawaiian flower necklaces.

Her cleavage open, her fake black eyelids fluttered, Clay felt weak, he noticed her foot was playing with his legs, how was that possible, she was over there and he here?

For an answer, 'Yellow rose of Texas 'hummed down from a mouth organ. It was a secret how she had done that, and she blew a kiss at him, and the red lips stuck to his right cheek.

Clay shook his head, there had to be weed in that cigar smoke, who knew what Johnny Christie smoked?

He felt invisible hands stroke his biceps, knew why she had sent for him, he was Clay, a legend already, the hero of The Alaskan Big Foot Tales, he had his colt six guns and holster, he was undoing his shirt buttons some and ogling Martha.

"*I am disgusted with you Clay AND THIS IS WHAT YOU THINK WHEN OGLING, and so our engagement is off, giggle.*"

"*Marry me then?*" *Fili Pek.*

"*Get lost Fili Pek giggle.*"

ANYWAY, at the dining table, Nathan noticed this imbecilic play by these two kinder garden escapees and interrupted from **jealousy,** he stuck his foot onto Martha's foot for foot play and guess what, he was an imbecile as forgot to take off his boot.

"Nice meal Martha," Nathan innocently fingering the heavy silverware, Texans made things big.

Clay kept looking at the stuffed bison head above the fireplace, it was huge, was it Tonka, had the Texans shot and stuffed Tonka and that would explain why he only saw visions of Tonka.

"You must excuse darling Clay as he clings to Native Legends such as Big Foot and baboons with red bums existing and shape shifting critters, giggle hoping Clay did shift into a more amorous mood just for me giggle and that was an Auroch and bought by Martha was that cow huge and Texans did things bigger."

The dining table was longer than usual, Martha's reason was she let her men after washing eat civilized here.

The plates bigger, the food portions bigger, the waiter the biggest cowgirl stuffed into a black frilly waitress suit. The men stuffed dollar bills into her garters and that kept her mummy happy.

"Glad you enjoyed, it was 12lb steaks and you left some Nathan," and all glared at the sheriff to watch him clean his plate Texan style.

Nathan felt his belly moving trying to shift the other 6lbs he had eaten nearer the exit for relief.

Clay's plate was sparkling clean, as no one noticed his new friend under the table helping him.

A chicken clucked by chased by the chef, a small African American imported from Detroit, a proper Texan chef did have the BIG TURKEY roasting by now.

The chicken jumped the table and mouth organ music filled the room, the lights went off and when they were back on Nathan's plate as empty. Someone could be heard eating on the roof, a banjo string twanged, sadly *a chicken clucked a last cluck.*

"Food keeps the cold Texan night away from places," mouth organ music was heard again.

Martha sighed, whoever was playing, "A Yellow Rose of Texas."

Our boys knew who was on the roof, **did you or are you keeping it a secret.**

And the lights went off and when they went back on only Nathan and Clay were at the table and at their feet camping gear and on the table a compass and map with X on it.

"I am coming also," it was the chef.

The lawmen looked at him, Nathan was incredibly happy, the man was smaller than him.

Clay saw himself carrying both so shook his head but did ask, "Why?"

"Yes why? I wanted to know our side."

"My name is Ragnar and a senior PhD student from the University of Iceland studying the paranormal, shape shifter to be precise and am taking odd jobs to pay my way across their trail, I cook well, you ate, you enjoyed, think of it, no more cooking or washing, I can bring my own dish washer," the smaller than Nathan man told them.

Raucous laughter came from above interrupted by mouth organ music.

The boys looked at each other, then the small man.

They shrugged shoulders a to say, "Why not?"

*

The morning they were woken by mouth organ music and the stink of a cigar with no window open.

After coughing and wandering blind to find the window

latch, they got fresh air.

"Tonka, gasp why have you dumped me here,' Clay breathing in fresh morning ranch smells.

Horse manure, long horn stuff, cooking smells, tobacco smoke and stiff necks from sleeping on a sofa pull out bed.

"Waffles and maple syrup," The voice chirpy, cheerful and Ragnar dressed as a chef.

The boys ate.

Ragnar brought thickest black coffee.

He dumped a menu; lunch was barbecued sheep in a Newman guacamole green sauce.

Then Kit threw in rucksacks from a window, piled a bazooka, two machine guns, bandoleers, grenades and acid reflex tablets, and a bible into this pile.

The lawmen looked at each other, their eyes said it all, "What have we got ourselves into?"

"Gee up sun's up,

Times a wasting," Kit and slid open French doors.

There were the original smiling horses chewing jerky, they now were Texan Horses.

Ragnar clicked his fingers and a smaller man than him appeared.

Nathan smiled very wide.

"He is Chinese," Clay as if that explained why he was so small.

Chinese spoken as the little fella cleared the room of what they needed and tied it to real mules not those Shetland Ponies pretending to be mules.

"He is called Kung Fu Jackie and is quick, did you notice he fleeced your wallets, ha, just joking," Ragnar but from now on the boys kept a hand on their cash while kung Fu Jackie was near, trouble was, he was so fast.

*

And the boys sat on the naughty horses with glints of hell in their eyes, the help on the Shetland ponies Clay asked, "She did be here to wish us luck if it were not for him."

"Yes him," Nathan.

As they turned their animals towards the main gate of the Silver Dollar Ranch

feeling alone, unloved, tearing into jerky imported caviar flavor, sniffing back sad funeral tears, they all looked out into the vast Texan Prairie the Comanche claimed as theirs all simultaneously said, "They did never find us to remember us on Remembrance Sundays," and a silence fell upon them as THE DEVIL TEMPTED THEM TO BUGGER OFF.

"I need my PhD on shape shifters and ghouls here about like those devil dogs," yes, it was the chef.

He was safe, these were lawmen wanting home to Alaska and Wendy Lou where they knew they were welcome heroes. He would not awake one morning heaven, Kung Fu Jackie, and I, me their guide Betty Lou, did drive temptation away.

Kung Fu Jackie did Kung Fu seriously.

And to avoid that made them remember Chelsea and Martha Lou cooking their meals, washing their draws and hero worshipping them without a trace of memory of Johnny Christie.

But they were wrong, this was Texas and knew how to say 'Adios,' for suddenly the whole population of Terlingua appeared in a dust storm of treks, wagons, 4x4's and suddenly it was, the silver dollar was only a mile from town.

The town band appeared and cheerleaders, mostly the girls from Chelsea's.

And behind was Martha and her crew.

In front was Chelsea Lou all smiles.

The press was here to.

The boys would be famous in Texas.

Already epitaphs were being written.

And so overcome were the heroes they never noticed the back gate open, and a RV drive out. It went unnoticed as the boys were using the front gate, just as well or the cigar smoke drifting from the driver's window did shatter their dreams of hero worship.

And the home on wheels had all the modern conveniences in it.

Was Madam Wendy Lou still in there?

Who was that other shadow in there, Cindy Lou?

Was that a Big Foot on the roof acting as the crow's nest giving a middle hairy finger at you?

You been eating too much Texan refried Beans extra chili and Newman Guatemala sauce friend.

*

"This is more like it 'Home on the range friend Clay," Nathan resting against his saddle watching Ragnar prepare dinner.

Clay began to retch as Ragnar skinned a skunk.

Nathan joined him, he was not eating skunk.

"You boys in Texas now, you eat on the range, that skunk caught way back in time, needs cooked, starting to smell, I go fry the beans and forgot, you want young girl postcards?" Kung Fu Jackie taking from a pocket a phone with a giant screen with girls winking at the boys.

"Fili Pek get down, get lost," as Fili Pek looked and got excited forgetting he was dead.

And Ragnar finished skinning the potatoes and turning them into Duchess Creamed Mash Twirls, he was a chef, what skunk, that idiot Kung Fu Jackie had some imagination and the heroes being hapless watching the sunset, listening to the calls of the wild, hungry coyotes, their lungs filled with desert flower essences that made them slightly hallucinate, believed the aspiring salesman selling postcards, hair cream, nose hair trimmers and young girl chat numbers, yes his name was Kung Fu Jackie as aspirer to be a World Wide renowned Television Chef.

And Jackie spread out a checkered tablecloth, big spoons, ketchups, and Duchess potatoes.

The boys looked eagerly for the main course, this had to be a side dish.

"What do you think I am, 'Wonder Chef from the Planet Kryptonite? We are in the middle of nowhere and you expect steaks, roast turkey, trimmings, and cool iced water, see this," and the annoyed chef copied the Big Foot on the roof of the RV. With a finger.

Jackie pouted his lips in agreement and joined the chef behind the bags, water barrels, tents, mobile latrine, walk in shower, radio television set and soon his and Ragnar's laughter reached the boys.

That was not all that reached them.

The smell of frying noodles and the sound of 'Judge Judy,' telling folks where they fools to make themselves fools on her show.

The boys looked at their empty plates and each other, slowly they filled with annoyance and Clay got up, then pulled Nathan up so he dangled first.

Just as well he did as a rattler slid under him.

Both men froze and did not move as the rattler bedded down under Nathan and still the smell of frying noodles reached them making them ravenous.

"If I drop you friend think you can stomp the rattler dead before deadens you?" Clay seeing roast snake on their campfire.

"Are you nuts best friend?" Nathan emphasizing BEST.

An hour passed.

"Best friend I need a pee," Nathan.

"Well just do not pee on the snake, it might reach up and bite me someplace Chelsea needs," Clay being careless and Nathan's eyes narrowed and, "I understand friend," and 'BEST' was missing.

Yes, Nathan understood, and we can suppose hanging there above a rattling would affect anyone.

Nathan peed seeing knowing soon only he did have working parts for Chelsea to make her laugh as she cooked pumpkin pie for him, whipped homemade ice cream, made a cocktail, and helped him drink it, their lips touching, their eyes, never mind, Nathan could dream.

"Rattle," the rattler went.

"I thought we were friends?" Clay realizing his mistake but too late.

The peeved rattler struck up and, "rattle," as Clay's guide blew the rattler of course so it bit Nathan's extra-large cod piece and was stuck.

"Help," Clay coughed.

"Oh, Chef help please," Nathan using the magic word and Chef appeared but seeing the snake disappeared.

THAT WAS IT.

An hour passed.

Jackie appeared with a long stick and prodded the rattler that of course got annoyed.

"Rattle," the reptile went and struck out at Jackie freeing itself from Nathan.

It then followed Jackie back to the kitchen quarters where the mayhem began.

"Quick Nathan, Tonka has told me to build up the fire, snakes hate fire," Clay throwing their paper dining plates onto their small campfire that radiated heat that brought the snake as Texan nights were COLD.

Nathan emptied Newman's Kindling Sticks onto the fire and just like that burst into flame and the light from the flames and the paraffin camp light illuminated a flying rattler coming their way.

"Run friend," Clay and being huge when compared to Nathan easily grabbed the later and dodged the snake.

"Are they idiots or trying to kill us, are they in the pay of the badmen, IS THAT A SECRET?" Nathan.

Clay after making sure the snake was not following went to seek his colts, but as he never wore them, had no idea where they had been packed.

But thought it a good idea he will wear them from now on.

"You two children, that is a rubber snake, we eat it tomorrow for breakfast, taste like chicken," Kung Fu Jackie picking up the lifeless snake going back to the kitchen area.

Nathan strapped on his tranquilizer pistol.

"The boys were armed, oh, Clay found his colts and a real sleeping skunk.

Explains why the boys ran into the prairie with an angry TEXAN BIG skunk chasing them.

Oh, real Texan men did have shot the skunk and told the chef that was lunch, but Clay was a pacifist and vegetarian.

How could these men shoot the angry skunk intent on scenting them?

By the way, Nathan ate whatever a girl cooked for him."

"You smell you boys need a bath next river we come to, just make sure no water moccasin snakes swimming," Jackie holding his nose.

But the boys were back, so was the skunk, it showed our two who was boss and where it was sleeping and them. It was a Texan skunk; they came on the big size and could wrestle.

"Alaska was never like this friend," Clay moaning.

Nathan produced two chocolate peanut butter bars.

"Here friend," and gave Clay his.

"Ah the smell of peanut butter brought that skunk out from the cozy place it snoozed.

"Here," Nathan throwing his bar at the animal.

"Fetch," Clay copying, and the skunk went away with the bars leaving nothing.

And the coyotes howled nearer.

The boys edged nearer to each other for comfort and warmth.

Those horses and ponies of theirs with the wicked glint in their eyes cuddled together also, and not for warmth either. *"Giggle."*

"Ah nicely roasted," Ragnar spitting Jackie in a teddy bear suit.

"He was Ragnar's hot water bottle and Jackie would be warm and cozy against the howling coyotes, as long as they kept the fire

up."

As they were falling asleep silence fell on the prairie.

Evil was about or something science had not dissected and classified.

It was hungry and wanted that snake slow cooking on the chef's fire. It had a name, Dolly and was a female, tough, mean, nasty and a vampire.

"It had red eyes, so must be evil but cats have green and yellow eyes so must be evil also? Giggle, I am just pointing it out."

"Rodeo King are we letting the Chupacabra pack loose as a diversion while the boys rustle Silver dollar cows?" Jesse puffing on a cheroot **so his eyes glowed red.**

Rodeo King swiped Jesse with his Stetson, "Not so loud, those lawmen will hear you or even a Silver Dollar cowboy watching their herd," Rodeo King and, *"was just an excuse to swipe Jesse who had been behaving lately so had had no reason for Rodeo King to beat the living daylights out of him.*

And Rodeo King breathed on his vape ***so his eyes glowed yellow*** *for the vape was full of vanilla essence.*

Jesse strained his neck closer to sniff the delightful smell and was swatted again with these words, "I wonder what gender you are cowgirl?"

Unknown to Rodeo King but known to us, *Jesse was wondering that also since his chance meeting with the bad corrupt lazy prairie burger eating deposed sheriff.*

*

"Moo," a thousand times so you understand this silver Dollar herd was big and mouth organ music played and guess what, it was the three Silver Dollar cowhands playing to settle the herd down and not him, *"Johnny Christie, giggle.".*

The cows smelt vanilla essence that unsettled them.

These cowhands dreamed of Martha's apple pies freshly

baked and left on the open kitchen windowsill for them to steal and eat **in** the haystack, sharing it with the Native American and Latino domestic staff for the cowhands taught them Texan ways, English, how to use a knife and fork, a Bowie knife for carving open pumpkins on Halloween, what where the best Clint Eastwood cowboy films and the domestic staff having been brought up proper would reply, "Eh?" And gesticulate with their hands they only spoke Spanish, Navaho, Comanche or Chinese and laugh amongst themselves at the horrid names they named the cowhands.

For instance, there was 'Hairy Nostril,' and 'Wee Willie Wonka,' that had a double meaning or 'Hairy Moons,' or 'The Green Giant', that had nothing to do with fairy tales and astronomy and just why were these polite girls using vulgar nicknames for these bowlegged cowhands?

*"Giggle, **it is a secret**."*

And Martha did sit on her porch in a rocking chair smoking a cigar knowing where her staff where, for the haystacks moved thus saving her cash installing security cameras, and Martha looked down at a spare mouth organ she held and started blowing it horridly.

Her cow dog wailed, her cat ran off, her pet buzzard flew away but her wizened nanny hitting ninety understood, so sighed and went to make Martha her hot milk toddy to help her sleep and keep the bogyman away.

And in the kitchen emptied half a quarter bottle of Chelsea's moonshine into the hot milk, yes that would put anyone to sleep and added a sleeping tablet, see Grandpa Smith was visiting tonight.

And while Martha dreamed of a mouth organ player, the nanny waved to a bunk house and a ninety-year-old ranch blacksmith hobbled over and in his hand the rest of that Chelsea moonshine.

"Bad nanny and bad grandpa is that anyway to treat Martha

who has a motto, 'no work, no pay, no pay, no food, no pay no bed,' so knew how to treat bad Martha who worked her staff into a nearby pioneer cemetery, giggle."

So, we see what the three cowhands put up with under Martha, long hours on the open range **with no female company.**

*

And Rodeo King knew the cows were his tonight as he had promised the three cowhands half a share per cow so they could ride into Mexico and live in cheap border motels full of girls selling postcards of Mexico.

Drink tequila and east the worm at the bottom of the glass as was full of vitamins.

Not see a horse again, not be lonely again, not be stuck with the company of bowlegged men on horses that stank of the prairie and have folks wondering.

Rodeo King knew green dollars talked for 'Money made the world go round," was his favorite song.

"Jesse go send in one dog," Rodeo King instructed his friend, no, man Friday, no, Jesse, yes, Jesse and the other bad men cleared away a bit.

"Me boss, why always me?" Jesse complained and was swatted.

It was a heavy whack so even the badmen cringed and looked away feeling sorry for Jesse and knew one day Rodeo king did ride his last sedated bull in a rodeo, they did feed that bull refried extra hot chili beans, laced with Jalapa Reso peppers, marinated in Scots red Chili, covered in a Paul Newman Guacamole sauce **so the bull did not taste** the hot stuff but certainly **feel the hot stuff were needed.**

Goodbye Rodeo King and who would replace him, **it was a secret** giggle.

And Rodeo King sprayed female Chupacabra essence onto

Jesse's retreating jeans about his moon.

The watching bad cowboys thought,

1) Jesse was to provide entertainment.
2) That was unfair.

But being mean bad men looked forward to option one.

"Here Dolly, beef jerky," and Dolly came forward and ate the jerky and started licking Jesse's legs either out of friendship or to get a taste of desert. Dolly had smelt the pong on Jesse's moons so was probably a gay Chupacabra.

The pack wanted jerky also moved closer.

The stench on Jesse's moons was getting them intoxicated in 'Le Amour' mood.

The circle of badmen watching got closer not to miss a single rip, bite, chew, and swallow.

BUT Jesse had a bag full of jerky, a big bag like chicken carcasses, entrails, whose, never mind **it is a secret**, stolen apple pies and water bowls filled with Chelsea's moonshine to make the devil dogs a bit more open to suggestion.

"Go kill the lawmen, ok?" Jesse suggesting.

The watching cowboys knew Jesse was smarter than their Boss to still be alive and earned their respect.

"Woof," Jesse speaking Chupacabra and trotted away waving for the pack to follow.

It was with red and yellow eyes, eyes with all the rainbow colors that followed Jesse to rip, tear and chew him up.

And Jesse sensing he was dinner speeded up, he ran for his life, but the cowboys thought he was just speeding up events, after all, Rodeo King was known not to have patience.

"This way boys," the later now spoke and repeated

himself often but the men were now following Jesse to see what he would do next?

Rodeo king drew his pistols behind the backs of his men.

He cocked his guns and JUST LIKE THAT HIS BAD MEN TURNED AND POINTED FORTY COCKED GUNS AT HIM.

Rodeo King **tittered** and jested, "Just making sure you were still fast boys," and put his guns away and when his men went back to following Jesse, gave them many middle fingers, raspberries, funny faces and showed his mentality.

Then Rodeo King made his way to the bribed 'Silver Dollar' ranch hands.

And at out lawmen camp Jesse stopped near a cactus and emptied another carrier bag of what the establishments in town put in the trash.

Flies swarmed upon him.

The Chupacabra pack swarmed upon what he had dumped.

The following badmen gaped open mouthed, Jesse was intact?

"Dolly, here fetch," and threw a strip of Dolly's favorite jerky into the lawmen camp.

'Fresh Louisiana prawn flavor,' and that brings the tale to the gripping part where the devil dog Chupacabra ran and jumped over the Nathan and Clay pushing their heads down.

They were lucky it was Dolly and not them thieving fingered ones.

Nathan's ten-gallon hat fell into the fire.

Screams were heard as the dog ran into the kitchen area and out again with a teddy bear in its mouth.

A wiggling cursing teddy bear trying to stick fingers in those yellow eyes.

But the devil dog was experienced, it just opened the jaws slightly and Kung Fu Teddy rolled a bit out then Kung Fu Jackie felt the jaws close again, tightly **over sensitive places.**

"Fili Pek come and save the dishwasher, Fili Pek where art thou?"

The monster dog could eat all the snakes and chocolate peanut bars it wanted; Nathan wanted his hat.

The devil dog could not eat all the peanut chocolate bars or what would they eat? Clay remembered when the horses ran off. "I am going get you dog," Clay and in his regulation Deputy navy long blue johns ran after the Chupacabra.

"Was my pin up insane, had Tonka possessed my handsome lad giggle? Fili Pek get here now."

"Wait for me," Ragnar afraid of the pitch dark of the prairie.

"I am alone, wait for me," Nathan following.

And a cactus followed them, silently leaving no exhaust, it ran on a portable electric battery.

Someone inside the blow-up cacti laughed, there was soft pitched laughter and squeals, a banjo played 'The Eyes of Texas.'

"Oh, Johnny your hair is dyed, giggle," and was that an Alaskan girl called Madam Wendy Lou who was a long way from Alaska and an R.V. with a Big Foot on the roof practicing the finger at any sound or movement.

Inside cooking smells smelt.

The Big Foot licked lips.

"Thyite jug," the critter said and translated, "What is good for Johnny is good for me, Prairie Maryland with fried banana, chips, eggs, gammon, fried tomato and lots coffee."

This Big Foot did not want to go back to freezing Alaska that got 90 days of sunshine. Why Johnny had offered it the job of night watchman and accepted, and the critter was happy and male, so what difference does that make.

It was related to male dogs, worms and amoeba that lived in sewage drains, it ogled, and Cindy Lou thought it was ogling the cooking, she was mistaken.

It was male and the sooner Johnny woke up he could stuff it inside a cardboard box and post it back to Alaska.

Where it could freeze.

And be happy for out of its deep fur pull out a purple bra and ogle it.

"And proves me correct, it was a male, giggle."

Anyway, away from Big Foot, our lawmen were chasing a Chupacabra with a small Chinese man in a teddy bear jump suit dressed for bed.

Character Update Rodeo King

"I was a rotten bully at school since there were only a handful of pupils Terlingua School that served as Primary, Middle and high Schools so was an easy thing to do to 'Beat the Living Daylights' out of smaller pupils, feeding well on apples, pears, pecan pie slices for the teachers by their pet pupils, Cowboy Stews, Chili dishes, Texan Twinkles, jalapeno stuffed peppers with meats and barbecue sauce, Easy Pork Posole in plastic containers, easy for me to sell back to the children or else I did 'Beat The living Daylights,' out of them and met Jesse whom I did that too often as he scampered behind me, getting under my legs tripping me up in front of young Martha and Chelsea so they tittered, giggled and made funny faces ending with nosy raspberries and a tongue stuck out at me.

Because I was in puberty, I loved all that attention from them and allowed them to walk over me in their sparkling white trainers.

More heaven as I looked heavenwards but that idiot Jesse

wanted to see so got in the way so saw nothing except the back of his head.

See, Jesse encouraged me to keep 'Beating the Living daylights' out of anything annoying me, like Jesse.

Yet I showed kindness to him by letting him scavenge the chocolate wrappings I dropped so he could lick the chocolate smudge left.

I wanted love, affection, worshipped by Martha and Chelsea and found rejection so swore to become 'RODEO KING,' the 'BADMAN KING.'

Met Chupacabra, ugly, mangy, scaly, blood suckers and knew my future lay with them.

"Why you want to ang about them ugly critter for?" Jesse being annoying so started the Stetson swatting and still swat him. He reminds me of a fly buzzing about you.

And never answered him as it was my secret and above my bed not images of The Virgin Mary, but drawings of Chupacabra and sneaky snaps shots of Martha and Chelsea as was in puberty.

"We going to kidnap those girls and have a servant each Rodeo King?" Jesse and was swatted away.

"Share and share alike amongst best friends Rodeo King," Jesse and for that beat the living daylights out of him.

Now I am older and meaner and hornier and still those girls shun me but got their attention rustling and stealing their valuables by using my trained devil dogs to do my dirty work.

"I do your dirty work too Rodeo King," Jesse much to close, what gives with this boy, so swatted and beat the living daylights out of him.

"Lovely," Jesse and knew then Jesse was not a real cowboy, badman, Texan or pioneer and never let him get close to me again.

"We are the best of friends Rodeo King?" Jesse jumping like a dog waiting for a stick to fetch.

"Yeh sure, now Jesse go into town and pull-down Chelsea's washing, then go to Martha's and swop the washing on the washing line there, understand, good, then return to Chelsea's and put Martha's washing up, good man, now go," and Jesse went to please me, caught both washing lines and got the daylights beating out of him, and earned a reputation as 'He who sneaks about washing lines.'

CHAPTER 7   KUNG FU JACKIE, DENISE?

Chelsea's budgie, they are big in Texas.

"What the greatest martial arts dishwasher to hit the 'Big Screens' demised, so if true cannot giggle, he was last seen in a teddy bear pajama suit in the mouth of a Chupacabra as its dinner."

"Friend I am saving you," Ragnar and was a lie and he could not run as fast as the Chupacabra so stumbled here and there down gopher borrows. Now one borrow has extended families of gophers living down there so Ragnar must have disturbed about a thousand when he fell flat on his face stumbling out of the latest borrow with these words, "I cannot save my friend Jackie as am completely lost," so was natural he screamed in a quiet voice as was knackered doing all that running, "HELP," and added "wheeze."

But those that heard were too busy to help for they were.

1] Clay

2] Nathan

3] A laughing cacti

4] Ragnar

5]   An RV with a supposed extinct Gigantopithecus at the

wheel.

6] Screams of terror from inside the RV

7 A herd of a thousand rustled stampeding cows making their way to Mexico.

8] A posse of disappointed badmen wanting to watch what Jesse did do next.

Disappointed as they had hoped to see Jesse chewed, bitten, snapped, torn asunder.

By the Chupacabra pack.

9] Jesse running for his life.

10] The pack of Chupacabra after the essence of Dolly on Jesse's moons, sprayed there by the man he hero worshipped.

11] Rodeo King trying to guide his petrified horse out of the lead of the horde of stampeding cattle.

1] "Br, these Texan nights are freezing," Clay forcing himself from a law man's duty to keep following Dolly.

Remember Clay only had on regulation navy long blue johns and needed band aid as in the cloudy moonlight had run into many a real cacti.

"Hey, I still have my colts on, why did not I think of this before, I am an American," and drew his colts and blazed where he heard slurping hyena giggles and a faint human voice calling, "Help," and "this mangy dog is for it when I am free, it is Chop Suey and besides the animal's breath stinks."

2] "Sometimes I wonder if doing the law man is worth it and one of those times is now," and stumbled into a moving cactus.

Angry banjo music greeted him.

"Titter giggle," a female was in the cacti and Nathan

recognized the giggle.

"Cindy Lou is that you?"

In response an arm of the cacti whacked him, and the cacti took off.

"Ouch," Nathan pulling thorns out of his cheeks and, "I am alone and afraid of the boogeyman in the dark so am running AFTER THAT CACTI FOR I KNOW Johnny Christy is in there and he can save me and **what I told is our secret."**

But ran into Ragnar who was covered in thousands of Prairie dog gophers annoyed at being woken out of their dream time, their time of never mind, so Ragnar was in trouble.

So, was Nathan now as the cute prairie dogs covered him.

"Clay best friend where art thou," and listened and heard gun shots so saying, "I will head for the sound of battle," and was some achievement walking like that blown up fake cacti as was covered from head to foot in prairie dog.

"I have recovered my breath so will follow the law and be saved," Ragnar covered in prairie dogs.

3] The laughing cacti was getting close to Clay so that is why HE inside stopped. He knew best not let Clay hear the tittering giggling coming from inside the cacti, especially since he was firing colts off.

He also had used his mobile and spoken gibberish to an ape of the roof.

"Come and pick me up, juicy watermelon in it for you," for Johnny Christy knew why walk when he could enjoy the home comforts of an RV.

5] We know all about the frolics of Ragnar.

6] The RV lurched dangerously as the ape at the wheel had never taken any driving lessons, so now was a good time to start and explains the female human petrified screams in the

RV.

"I am going to kill you Johnny," Madam Wendy Lou bounced about in the RV.

7] "Moo," a thousand times as scared cows came their way as a pack of horny Chupacabra had tried to eat them, but taking on a thousand cows was a fool hardy thing, so the pack of Chupacabra were content in staying at the back of the herd laughing like hyenas and saving face.

8] The posse of badmen caught up with Jesse and rested their horses. A silly thing to do as a stampeding herd was heading down on them, but one said, "Hey someone is shooting at me."

It just takes one then the pack notices and thinks collectively.

"Take that back whoever is shooting at me," and a badman blazed away into the night.

Soon eighty guns blazed, see each man had two pistols so that means there still were the original forty badmen.

9] Jesse had reached the forty badmen and passed them and puffing and wheezing had to about turn in front of Rodeo King who was unable to guide his scared horse to safety.

10] The Chupacabra pack liked it amongst the forty badmen whom they knew so rested and did not cause any trouble, "do you believe me, giggle?"

A horse is a horse and does like take kindly to Chupacabra stink, so bronco pranced they went.

Forty horses and forty Chupacabra avoiding them, oh yes there was trouble, and the badmen blazing away and Clay blazing at them.

"Kit, tell the men to open fire," Martha awakened by all the commotion. Beside her granny nanny serving hot chocolate and jam doughnuts.

In the distance grandpa blacksmith sneaking back to the

bunk shed. He was smiling so was glad of the interruption as Granny nanny would keep him up all night, he wanted his bed, why he was an old bent arthritic Mannie.

He could do with a teddy bear pajama jump suit to keep his bones warm.

Now Terlingua was only a mile down the prairie and the town was awake.

Men, women, and toddlers were strapping on their guns.

The aliens had arrived on the prairie and the men of the Silver Dollar doing night watch had taken them an all by themselves Texas Style.

They needed help but being Texans would not ask, they did go down with their boots on and a yellow rose in their teeth.

"Room," went Chelsea's 4x4 as she packed the back with serving girls, moonshine, and jerky.

HELL, NOT ALIENS HAD ARRIVED ON THE TEXAN PRAIRIE.

"Sheriff that you?" Madam Wendy Lou asked from the stopped RV. The ape was having second thoughts about one watermelon for this 'hellish' night work.

The ape was on the mobile demanding three from Johnny who was arguing back, Johnny knew the ape needed taken down a peg or two, there was only one boss here and it was him not some Big Foot that was asking to be stuffed into a cardboard box and posted back to Alaska where watermelons were absent apart supermarkets.

This ape better not figure that out or there did be

break ins in supermarkets.

"Watermelon thief strikes again," the paparazzi did print.

"Yes, my darling let me in," Nathan doing sweet talk.

Madam Wendy Lou looked about for a moving cactus,

seeing none opened a door and Nathan staggered in.

He was followed by Ragnar who knew the law did save him.

"S**t man, what the hell have you brought into the RV?" Wendy Lou dusting off prairie dogs.

With a kick she closed the RV door and heard knocking on it from outside.

"Whose there?" She asked.

Just knocking so flinging off a prairie dog from her hair she opened the RV door with a loaded shot gun pointed out into the night.

Thousands of prairie dogs seeking safety from a stampeding herd of cows that were knocking at the door.

With a kick she shut the door, but the prairie dogs were quicker, they all got in.

The RV started up again, that ape at the wheel was smiling, he had got five watermelons out of Johnny.

As for Johnny he had given in because bullets zinged everywhere making him dance.

"I am out of here," a female who unzipped her cacti from within and Cindy Lou jumped out only in mm, lingerie, no that is too far, a teddy bear jump suit, no too hot in the cacti, swim wear, yes bright orange swim wear.

LIFEGUARD was printed across the chest.

The RV stopped and she climbed up the roof not liking what she saw at the windows,

PRAIRIE DOGS, millions of them for they
breed quickly in the heat.

Johnny was gaping, his beautiful RV was shredded inside out by PRAIRIE DOGS.

He needed to bribe that ape with honey melons to sweep up the pooh, disinfect the carpets, wash the bedding, and dry it. Thus, the ape was saved being stuffed into a cardboard box and did like to see Johnny try as that ape was nine feet tall, but Johnny had his ways and always won.

"Maybe not this time giggle."

"Cindy Lou, are you in there?" Clay asked at the RV.

"No, it is an A1 robotic look alike," Johnny lying to save his skin as Clay still held smoking guns and they might have been spent so if so, Johnny could relax, he did just have to fight a ferocious jealous murderous Native American because that was his woman in there under a moving carpet of PRAIRIE DOGS.

Not to worry, Rodeo King was approaching, and Jesse and the King were gyrating at the pelvis twisting this way and that for way out of HELL.

And Jesse unknown to him had jumped onto the back of his horse.

Jesse had true grit and knew how by watching Cowboy Movies.

Rodeo King never heard or felt him but did start to smell that essence that made him twist this way and that.

It was when Jesse put his hands about his midriff to better hold on, he KNEW.

"GET OFF," was Rodeo King's reaction and looked down at those hands to unclasp, silly man so only saw the RV at the last moment and his horse being sensible stopped dead, sending Rodeo King flat as a pancake against the RV side.

"Grump," or something he mumbled as he slid to the ground senseless.

And Jesse rode off into the night.

The forty badmen rode by blazing away filling the RV with ventilation holes and the prairie dogs knew it was time to get back into their borrows, but not before running amok on

Johnny Christy, covering him in fur, fleas, pee and pooh so he stunk and any cooking lessons with the girls was 'OUT THE WINDOW.'

Then the thousand cows ran over him, knocked over the RV by sheer numbers so the open door the prairie dogs and exited fell across Clay and Johnny.

Both men looked at each other knowing they had felt like poohing themselves seeing the pearly gates of heaven and just how lucky they were the RV door had been opened, or they did been flattened good.

"There are my cows, let us get them boys," Martha and led her men off after them blazing away by herself.

"Aliens," the towns folk and blazed after her.

"Well, hello all, cold beer and hot chili refried beans to be drank and eaten, and toilet paper also as town is a long way off after eating my extra hot chili beans made that hot so you got to drink more to cool the throat," Chelsea.

"Yes, she was some businesswoman, perhaps maybe the next Pr4esident giggle."

"Give me a triple," and was Kung Fu Jackie emerging from the dust a forgotten character, forgotten for what is there to write about being carried halfway across Texas by a Chupacabra wanting to chew, rip and bite you up as dinner?

Nothing much, except Dolly knew when to drop him and get out of the way of a thousand angry cows.

Yes, with these words Kung Fu Jackie saw heaven, "I am free now to Kung Fu that smelly dog, hey the ground is trembling, what the hell?" A thousand cows stampeded about him and missed him as he was so small.

And explains why he was covered in dust needing a triple shot of moonshine.

"Someone plays the fiddle and let us line dance," one of Martha's men.

And the till on the 4x4 grew hot from opening shutting and Chelsea grew richer.

Character Update Jesse

"I am a Texan, a badman of the prairie and ride with Rodeo king, King of Texan Badmen and can eat and hold down the hottest chili Corn Carne and hold in my meal and not need a Terlingua latrine, a hole in the ground the Town council pays a digger to dig. The job was mine till I met rodeo king and graduated into a taker, stealer, thieving varmint, rustler and all round BADMAN.

I love Rodeo King and have since I first saw him, my Badman hero that takes no c**p from no one.

Who cares about Martha and Chelsea, Rodeo King has me, I carry six guns, have a Shire Horse to make me look bigger and important and know all the dirty on folks as do all Rodeo Kings paperwork.

I often wonder about me and see, washing I kept tucked in a boot, and never let any of Rodeo King's badmen friends see or they did pin me on a cactus and fill me with lead.

It is our secret; never tell Rodeo King, he did feed me the Chupacabra in a mild chili sauce in case it gave them the runs.

A secret right?

CHAPTER 8   PEACE ON THE PRAIRIE

"Hell fire, I will fire them all when I get back to Terlingua," Martha sitting on her horse viewing her cows drinking from the Rio Grande.

"These your cows madam?" And Martha looked down into the brown eyes of a Big Bend park Ranger, hell fire he was better looking than Clay, what where these feeding these young bucks?

Behind him was a motley crew of tourists, many holding canoe, raft paddles, punctured big black car wheel tubes, wet cameras, soaking socks, larger than life catfish, a mallard duck, and no idea how it got here, and parts of motorcycle mountain bikes, pots and pans and hands suggesting payment for damage.

"No, they are Rodeo Kings, and his ranch is a mile yonder there," Martha lighting a cigar lying through her size 48 DD bra supports.

As she watched the lynchers become smaller on the prairie she out loud, "Cannot fire the c***s as there is no one else to hire," and started singing a Dolly Paton song, "The Best Little Whore House in Texas," and was not thinking of Chelsea's eats but her own Castle, her folly on the Texan Prairie, "See Martha getting a hot toddy from Granny Nanny every night put her to sleep while a stone throw away bunk houses full of men covered in blisters on the moons, blisters on the soles, from horse riding, hands so rough they did not need gloves to mend wire fencing that was not needed as Martha knew Texas reached Washington D.C., everything was Texan so why fence? Hands so calloused that if they gently stroked Martha's delicate facial skin did skin her alive leaving her smashing all the mirrors she owned.

Yes, Martha was a lonely woman inside, *"and feel deeply for her for here is my help Fili Pek sneaking up on my transparent legs pretending he is a spirit dog, so I pat and hug him, and why I am lonely for Clay is the only man I am waiting for to come my side, get off me Fili Pek, fetch, giggle."*

"He Rode All the way to Texas," Martha sang as a thousand cows followed her home.

*

"What is that noise, can a copy of 'Jesse James 'not get any sleep, where is my Boss Rodeo King to investigate the clamoring for justice and that word JUSTICE makes me sneak under the crack of the back door of my bunk house and get caught," Rodeo king trying to escape the mob come up from the Rio Grande.

"Your cows damaged the Balmorhea State Park Rio Condo Fast Food Takeaway, pay up or else," the owner of that takeaway swinging a lynching lasso and added, "you smell bad".

"Your cows had the runs and polluted my spring onion crop I water," another, a woman from the orient and showed Jesse where she did put her soil covered garden trough and added, "Chupacabra scent you or skunk?".

Jesse covered his moon and gulped, "Boss, Rodeo King please save me" he squeaked; but in his heart he knew Rodeo King did beat the daylights out of him for wakening him,

"Whose Rodeo King," a Mescalero Apache Native American dressed in photographic wet soggy wear pointing at Jesse's scalp with a Bowies knife, rubber of course for the tourists or he did lose his Busking License and added, "you smell like a shape shifter, you need burned at the stake."

"Pay me and not in beads, I want dollars," a Chisos Native American and threw a lance that LANDED BETWEEN Jesse's legs, so he swallowed as he did not want to be laughed at by the girls in the Purple Haze and added, "you belter buy men's pads as you are not house trained, phew."

Chelsea did never let him in her upper-class establishment although she was seen to take dollars from the cellar door from him in the dark, she was some businesswoman.

"Wait friends, does Rodeo King own the cows?" A Comanche just saving Jesse's neck and added, "your moons, keep them away from me, you been sitting in cow pie or something?".

"Rodeo King, he went that away and has a saddle bag of cash," Jesse lynching his boss, "a man's love for his friend goes only so far, especially one who never read the BIBLE, so did not believe in 'There is no greater love than to give your life for a pal,' as Jesse remembered all the swatting and beatings he took from his Boss, so his Boss could get lynched Texan style with an extra-long rope from a bigger tree.

"That mean must be more cash here," a tourist angry her planned wedding on a raft on the Rio Grande as it went through rapids had been ruined and started ransacking Rodeo King's bunk house with a bandana covering her nose as Jesse smelt of Chupacabra essence still, "what are these?" She asked holding up 'Shaun the Sheep' shaped woolly Y fronts as Texan nights get cold.

"And to laughter and scorn Jesse shrunk to a smaller size so slithered towards the back door.

"Money," a stupid tourist not realizing if he kept silent it would all be his, as he held up a wad of money and gagged as the smell of Jesse's moons reached up his nose.

"Monopoly money as Rodeo King loved that game as he dreamed of becoming rich and President of America living in a 'Rodeo's Tower,' in Houston but it was gloomy in the bunk house so the mob pulled another's hair, poked someone else eyes, gave the opposition thick cauliflower ears, some bleeding lips, and many dentists richer than what they were, over fake MONOPOLY MONEY, giggle, here Fili Pek your wages giggle."

"I cannot see a thing," a tourist who had lost her glasses and most of what she wore and lit a match to light up a paraffin light as Rodeo King still lived in the Wild West.

Everyone stopped fighting and ogles, yes even the women out of jealousy for this girl was a stunner.

"Titter the girl and burning her fingers on the match dropped it and the paraffin light so "FIRE," was repeated and the bunk house emptied.

"Look other bunk houses," a driver of a Greyhound Bus whose bus needed a repaint job as was the victim of a thousand passing long horns.

"Tonka has blessed us," a Comanche doing a war dance that led him to the door of one, and quick as a lighting flash was inside and locked the door.

That started a mad rush for the other bunk houses and those that were kicked out by those inside, well went nuts, they tore up the desert flowers with their teeth, gnawed wooden white flaky fencing as Rodeo king was a lazy bugger, ransacked the barn of hay, knocked over the water tower, then set alight to the other bunk houses with these words, "Roast in there," then noticed that poor defenseless woman who had dropped the match.

My, in the burning bunk house glares she was pretty, and she saw the ogling maniacally look in the mob eyes, so knowing where Terlingua was, and being the High School best sprinter and long-distance runner, bolted.

"Look she is getting away," one of the maniacal idiots.

"What do we do? She will tell the law," another fool.

"I hear two famous lawmen are in Terlingua," another having read the newspaper.

"After her, I am not spending time in Alcatraz."

"And all they did wrong was ogle, arson, robbery with violence, and believed many had been roasted while in fact all got out the HANDY BACK DOOR, giggle."

*

"Johnny Christy had been visited by KARMA, what goes round comes round, giggle but I still love the man even if he stank of a thousand cows definitely not house trained, giggle."

He watched the RV drive away with the faces of two men at the back window, and out of respect for Johnny gave the middle fingers lower down unseen.

Terlingua was only a mile away, a cold dark night with rattlers slithering about.

An ape still drove the RV waiting to be bribed to come back and pick up Johnny Christy and the ape blew 'God Only Knows,' as had watched Johnny play.

And Johnny knew secrets we did not know, and taking from a back pocket an inflatable bouncing rabbit and pressing a button it blew up, and with a "Yippee Yahoo," he was away, and just how in heck did an inflatable rabbit fit in a back pocket, and more rubbish was catching up on the RV, and that is one of Johnny's secrets **that he will not tell you.**

As Johnny passed the RV windows, he did not hide the

middle finger from the boys at the back, or scowl at the girls on the side windows or show the ape **a postage stamp**.

The ape grew small and feared, it did not want to go back to Alaska so turned left into the Prairie, the stupid mangy beast.

"Let go the wheel," Cindy Lou blinding the ape with what Dolly Paton has in an effort to get the wheel but failed.

"Strawberry Ice in the fridge," Wendy Lou standing places an ape did like normally but still the ape refused to let go the wheel.

"I am a Native American Olympic Wrestler," Clay and the girls tittered, and the ape let go off the wheel to wrestle Clay out of his navy-blue regulation Long Johns.

And the driverless RV headed to Canada at 100 mph as a girl's shoe had come off a foot and got stuck on the gas pedal.

"We are Goma's, someone save me," Cindy Lou fainting across the wheel.

"I want to live; someone save me Wendy Lou swooning across Cindy Lou.

"Tyree Tuyet," gibberish from the ape translated," I want to live too," and opened the RV door and jumped out holding navy regulation long johns that parachuted out, so the ape did not break its neck but was blown away.

"Hopefully out of this Texan tale, giggle."

"SKIN WALKER RANCH," a sign passed this way, "TERLINGUA THE OTHER WAY," a sign passed also.

And a small man being so small was able to go under the pressed bodies on the drivers seat and retrieve the female shoe with these words, "Now I will be a hero and have two cooks to show me how to fry Texan beans, when the lights are off," but the girls woke and saw Clay trying to find clothes that did fit him, but he was taller than Johnny Christy so found none.

"Tonka what do I do?" Clay as the two girls advanced upon him.

And the question was, "Did they have a driver?"

The driver needed many cushions to sit on to see out the driver's window.

He also needed longer legs to reach the pedals.

He also could do with longer arms to reach the gear stick.

That answer your question.

*

And the sun was coming up on Terlingua town as a dirty unwashed drunk crowd headed down High Street.

A 4x4 drove into the back of Chelsea's and the girl herself got out heaving a canvas bag down into the cellar where she unlocked a padlock that allowed her to descend another flight of stairs, and after three more padlocks opened, she must be thirty feet down, and here a safe she deposited her well was tours, cash.

"Boss Chelsea, we need more drink to work," a missing resident of Terlingua and nobody missed him as he was a town drunk, an annoyance, a panty line thief, a pest wanting a drink out of you, a Peeking Tom who watched you bake so knew when to steal your apple pie cooling on the windowsill.

Chelsea spoke into a mobile and one of her girls appeared and a dumb waiter opened with cool XXX that was drank down by a small army of missing town drunks from Texas.

And many had leprous sores as mining mercury is dangerous.

Terlingua still had mercury and Chelsea and her girls knew and these drunkards who happily drank her moonshine and mined away without kitchen rubber washing up gloves on to protect their hands, or gas masks that cost money to protect their tobacco ravaged lungs.

Chelsea was some businesswoman.

Never mind the missing town drunks were going out the way they dreamed off.

They had waitress service.

*

An RV drove into Terlingua steered by only gassed by a small man at the pedals.

A small man about to be lynched for the RV was heading straight for Chelsea's where the mob was heading to for a 'hair of the dog,' and eventually become more free labor in Chelsea's mercury mine.

What could slow down the RV, the thrown of bodies trying to squeeze into Chelsea's swing front doors?

No, Chelsea's girls were exiting the back door with jars of moonshine, see how handy back doors were?

And forty-gun men, badmen arriving looking for Jesse to make him their new Boss did not stop the RV, they had been riding all night, were dirty, thirsty, and sleepy and headed to the Purple Haze were a few shots of Chelsea's moonshine sold here would revitalize them a few hours.

Yes, they had a future, in a mercury mine.

And Chelsea got about, she sold her liquor to the Purple Haze at discount, and they were happy to buy especially with forty badmen to fill the bar up and empty the casks.

Who did stop the RV.

Where was Clay.

Giggle and laughter came from the cooking area of the RV as Clay was taught how to knead pasty with the girls, *"Oh Yeh?"*

Where was Martha, you were needed here but she was absent and lynching granny Nanny back at her ranch as she had discovered what went into her nightly toddy, for Grandpa

Smith the blacksmith had been careless and left her half-drunk toddy glass and bottle.

"I am your nanny so hang him not me," Granny Nanny pointing at Grandpa Smith.

"Me, what did I do wrong Miss Martha?"

"You annoyed me," Martha thinking of nothing else to say but revealing she was a tyrant as we already guessed who paid her cow hands peanuts not dollars.

"Who did stop the RV giggle?"

And a bouncing rabbit neared with a Johnny Christy playing a mouth organ and banjo and how he did that without being bounced off is a secret, why this man remember was one of the country's best secret agents and full of c**p.

Would he get to the driver's seat and push Nathan down on the brake pedal saving Nathan from a lynching?

And a Gigantopithecus otherwise that ape or that Big Foot was blowing in on navy blue regulation long johns, would the ape land on the driver's window and having long arms reach down and pull on the hand brake? Just remember it had just completed driving lesson one and had no idea what a hand brake was but did see itself being blown into the mob who shouted, "we can skin it for the nights are cold," and takes one, "yes, a new blanket for the nights is cold," and "rubbish, I can mount the head over the bar," Chelsea from a hidden loudspeaker.

And the ape feared for its precious fur and as it huffed and puffed into the long johns failed to change directions.

"Hr. kufis Korf," left its big lips that translated, "mummy."

So, who would stop the RV putting a mob into hospital and who would pay the hospital bills for the U.S.A. does not have a National Health?

It was Rodeo King who no one had bothered to peel off the side of the RV when the cows stampeded earlier on.

Well, he peeled himself off now and screamed a lot as he went under the RV wheels, but Texan men are tough so was unharmed but shaken so staggered of to the Purple Haze.

"Hey, look our old Boss, let us lynch him," just takes one.

"He pays well," a waitress in the 'Purple Haze' objecting.

And they argued yea or nay to lynching Rodeo King the bad man king and being that walked into the bar tall and ready for his High Noon.

He pulled out his pistols and twirled them Texan style full of True Grit.

Amid many gunshots, screams and "I missed him," "Anybody get killed?" "Where did he go?" The Rodeo King ran out of that bar knowing he was not welcome there right back into the path of the RV, so he was hit and flattened the front window and sort of slid and blew into the driver's seat.

Below him Nathan got bored pressing down the gas medal, besides his back ached and needed stretched, so he did that and stared into the glazed eyes of Rodeo King, I mean would not you be dazed and glazed after being hit square on by a 40-ton RV.

"I am arresting you again man who is not my friend and where is my friend Clay, never here when needed?" Nathan and being a lawman always kept a spare handcuff somewhere.

And the RV came to a stop in the rumble of Chelsea's.

Well done the driver of that RV.

Just as well the lynchers lay moaning about the street.

And Chelsea was under the floorboards furious and being down there did see the funny side of things for she was a Texan woman, she knew she had willing free hands to build her a bigger Gentleman's Club and did call it the Cattle Association Club."

She also knew her mine tunnels extended far and wide,

like into Martha's disused copper and mercury mines, she Chelsea knew with free labor the mines did be profitable again, and she was right so with a waitress and drinks tray got her miners to clear rubble as she did not want to dirty her frillies she escaped hunger, oxygen deprivation, hands mistaking her for a light switch, hands knowing that was Chelsea so escaped KARMA.

"And would the towns folk build statues either end of High Street to our lawmen, you bet they would giggle."

And a bouncing rabbit bounced over the rumble and the moaners thought a Greek deity had come visiting so did not tremble for they were Texans and wanted the secret of that bouncing rabbit that bounced away to meet Chelsea when she emerged, and how did Johnny know where she was, well he was a womanizer and knew where his woman were, Chelsea his woman, well somewhere else was needed when the RV got hot and stuffy and full of women smells and the latrine blocked, well that Johnny got about, better lock up your own girls, hire security guards, nasty guard dogs, even Kung Fu Jackie as he came cheap.

And where were Kung Fu and his Boss Chef Ragnar?

Exhausted as having walked the mile to Terlingua, look they were kitchen staff, folk that sampled the trifle cream, the whipped cream in the asparagus soup, the cream and butter whipped up heated to pour over the crayfish, the folk that sampled the Irish Creams so by the nights end were useless except to burp and fall asleep.

Have pity on them, nibbled by thousands of prairie dogs, gored by a thousand cows, bullet creases all over their clothes that now were tatters, men fearing what was coming behind them, a mob of angry tourists suffering like them, a mom intent on lynching Rodeo King and behind them Jesse who wanted to say a final goodbye to the man he thought he loved, Rodeo king, and out of the town latrine emerged a large weighty individual, that sheriff.

"Cur what have I missed?" The sheriff suffering the jitters from too much moonshine and showing potential as a miner.

"Out of my way overweight man," Kung Fu forgetting what polite words where, besides the man smelled bad after sleeping the night in the latrine and flies buzzed him, roaches plagued his worn-out boots, a vulture waited patiently on a telephone pole, and a big fat fly landed on Jackie's lips, a roach ran up his ripped teddy bear leggings into his Micky Mouse printed shorts and was a hungry roach, the fly pregnant and laid live babies,

So, no wonder Jackie went insane and blamed the man in front of him so gave a free lesson in Kung Fu, then noticed the badge, "Oh dear who have I knocked senseless?" And did the wise thing, cleared off.

"Hello, whom do I have the pleasure in saving today?" Ragnar coming from Iceland did not leave stranded strangers to the elements but took them into the barn to get well, and earn their keep milking at 4 a.m., washing out the cowsheds, then feeding the cows hay, leading the cows to the pastures and cooking breakfast for the host, to start earning your keep till you were fit to leave.

But the corrupt sheriff was saved earning his keep in the kitchen area peeling potatoes into fries and baking Gofer Pies as that ravenous vulture flew down and carried him aloft.

A hundred yards up the vulture decided the meal was to heavy so let the meal go, besides vultures ate dead critters and after falling from that height the sheriff did be dead, tenderized, a vulture's delight, besides this was Chelsea's pet bird who remembered the hot cheroots this human threw it as treats thinking the bird stupid enough to eat.

Yes, the bird remembered this human as the bad man who offered it pizza slices and threw the slices under buses.

Yes, the vulture remembered this large human as he who took pot shots at it.

Revenge was here, karma and down fell the overweight man.

But had a soft landing on Kung Fu Jackie knocking him senseless.

And on High Street Nathan kept high kicking Rodeo King to jail, and not a member of the mob shouted, "Our hero," but "there is the twerp who flattened Chelsea's."

And he had left the RV door open and a mountain lion looking for her boyfriend to see if he was safe entered.

The giggling tittering ended in the kitchen area and the RV windows were opened and Cindy and Wendy Lou jumped out.

"Cur this was worth getting my bones crushed by that 40-ton RV," one of the flattened mobsters seeing the girls indecently dressed as cooking lessons is hot work.

Then Clay ran out the main door with the lion after him.

"Cur is that what a Native American looks like, naked?" Yes, a female mobster and glared away.

And Jesse arrived looking for Rodeo King to see if he was alive so he could breathe easy. He feared Rodeo King did fill him with lead from a guilty conscious.

And made his way to the Purple Haze where soon, "Hail Rodeo Jesse, King of the Bad Men," was heard AND HEARD BY Rodeo King in the jailhouse. Yes, IF he ever escaped Jesse better fear that lead coming his way.

And as Nathan was shutting the jailhouse door a naked Clay followed by a mountain lion ran by him.

Quick thinking Clay locked himself in the jail with Rodeo King who decided to stare at the floorboards rather than a naked Native American.

That means the mountain lion was outside with Nathan.

"Nice pussy cat," Nathan tried just before the cat pounced upon him and it was bloody, painful as the pet lion licked him into laughter.

Two boyfriends were better than two.

And an RV was heard to start up as mouth organ music was heard.

RV exhaust filled the jailhouse almost killing all inside.

And where was the RV heading, only Johnny Christy knew but it did stop for two hitching hiking girls, see Johnny was hungry and needed a curry, cold caramel drink, mushroom soup, and strawberry trifle, "Stuff the refried beans every day, a man needs a change of diet or comes down with scurvy."

"Who will cook for us friend?" Nathan and he and Clay looked at Rodeo King and stripped him good as he was a big man whose denim jeans although on the tight side, just fitted Clay and no more.

And with a yelp Clay pulled up the zip.

And that is how Rodeo King escaped police custody as while frying up the beans heated them and set them ablaze, so the jailhouse burned down.

And the cool Texan breeze blew the sparks onto every house in Terlingua, and they all burned down.

Yes, statues did be erected either end of High Street for the law men as well as lynching poles.

And as air ambulances arrived to take the injured mobsters away, the injured remembered who to LYNCH. And seeing the town derelict the Chupacabra ran wild, opening fridges and spoiling what was inside.

Yes, statues would be erected to those lawmen who are buried in the pioneer cemetery yonder, and did not mention how the lawmen died?

"Do they mean our boys?"

Character Update a Rotten sheriff

I went to the same adobe school in Terlingua as Rodeo King and he took my Texas Toast Garlic Bread off me, with these words, "What are you going to do about it overweight boy?" And sneered showing sparkling white teeth, then pinged the garlic bulbs right into both eyes.

At that moment I knew I did have to serve him or starve.

And when we grew up the job of sheriff became open and the girls were busy, Martha posing for magazines as a successful cowgirl in short denim cowgirl riding skirts, riding boots, and holding a whip, and not forgetting the pink Stetson and gold handled colts.

Chelsea, she was busy posing cardboard legs for the other type of magazines folk read behind the morning newspaper at breakfast table.

And the folk of Terlingua were busy preparing for The World Chili Day Heads Contest every Saturday November and the Green Living Day celebrating green living in the Chihuahuan Desert, now that is something as is SAND.

Then the Day of Dead parties and that is when I moved into the sheriff's office and became as rotten sheriff always in the morning diner saying hello to folks, there for morning coffee and doughnuts to say hello to folks, there at mid-day to eat eats, like Green Chili Brunch Bake a ground up sausage bake cooked with Worcestershire sauce, and there again for afternoon High Teas, drinking tea and eating Triple Layered Chocolate peanut cake so there was none left for anyone else, so they ate ordinary chocolate cake but still said hello to their overweight sheriff who was to overweight to stop the townsfolk doing what they wanted, 'LIVING THEIR WAY.'

Jaywalking, driving through nonexistent traffic lights, not arresting town drunks as he was one, and that suited

Chelsea as her fine whitewashed house with pink curtains and chickens in the garden was making the XXX.

And suited Martha as she knew her lonely cowboys needed the weekend to raise hell in Terlingua.

It made folk wary of her seeing her as a powerful woman with an army of cowboy drunkards.

So, they let the overweight sheriff get more overweight and when they caught Rodeo King rustling, did lynch him also Texas style, with the Terlingua Pipe Band, the picnic area opened for families, and the biggest ever tree to hang them from so all could see them lynched for miles.

And the rope on the overweight sheriff did break with his weight and they did decide to jail him for life, except the jailhouse had this handy back door he could vamoose out of and come back from the entertainment establishments and sleep it off, repeatedly.

There are perks to being an overweight sheriff on the take.

CHAPTER 9 SKIN WALKER RANCH, TERLINGUA STYLE.

Do Icelanders all look like Ragnar, well, he looks like he got off a flying saucer, and are those XXX empties? Is he the secret tippler and got that way from tippling too much.

There is a famous ranch in cowboy far-away lands that is always investigated for strange phenomena.

And strange phenomena were coming to the ranch.

"Well sheriff getting these baying hounds to track down Rodeo King is a good idea," Clay lying as the hound bayed all day and night, so Clay was in danger of sleeping in the saddle and falling off with a thud.

Nathan said nothing, it had been Martha's idea and they were her hounds, and hoped Clay did not notice her wink and moon pinching motions when she gave Nathan the leads, but he did so they were no longer best of friends.

And Clay hoped Nathan did not walk out the back door and see Martha smooching him a long time, so when she parted Clay was dizzy from her perfumes and was able to breathe again and she no longer pressed against his chest with those massive 48 DD appendages.

But a small shadow belied a small jealous man watching from the shadows and YES, they were no longer best of friends.

And Clay looked behind him at their growing baggage train.

Chef Ragnar was not being taught how to slow cook without a slow cooker in the middle of nowhere, and only Kung Fu Jackie knew how to cook Texas Pulled Pork Sandwich and **being a secret sorry you are not getting to know.**

"But I know and am telling, for on one of those donkeys a mobile solar battery and slow cooker, why Chef Ragnar even brought Mr. Sparkle washing up liquid and rubber gloves for the dish washer that was complaining he was no longer a dish washer with these words, "I no longer wash dishes understand Chef Ragnar?" Whose head Jackie had between his thighs drumming the head soi it nodded in agreement.

No one disagreed with Kung Fu Jackie when he was in one of his mood's giggles, oh Fili Pek go save Ragnar or the boys will go hungry, and the darling appeared as an orb and frightened the waste out of Jackie who let go of Ragnar and ran off into the dark rattler infested prairie.

Would he get bitten a thousand times, collapse and be eaten by army ants by morning, his bones chewed by coyotes and his innards trailed across the sky by buzzards, so they spelt, "Eat at Jackie's."

Ah now we see why he is no longer a dishwasher but an entrepreneur from the orient giggle."

Behind them on a donkey was Grandpa Smith to shoe

any lame horses and next to him Granny Nanny to keep the old man warm at nights for Texan nights are cold.

And Clay realized that extra smooch behind Martha's ticket booth to buy tickets to enter her castle was to blind him to the truth, THIS WAS A SUICIDE MISSION, Martha did not want the elderly folk back and only one of them.

He looked at Nathan, who wanted a battery-operated dwarf on their mantel piece when Martha had a real man, him, yes, the best of friends.

Yes, Martha had in fact stuffed retirement home brochures down Clay's front, so his eyes widened, and a Cheshire cat grin spread on his face.

"He was an unfaithful dirty minded Native American giggle."

And behind them on a mountain tricycle an ape that played soothing mouth organ music to calm the equines.

"I will give you back your Alaskan woman and put in good reports to my BOSS on you two lawmen if you take the ape of my hands, just keep him outdoors as he knows what a hole in the ground is for, but not how to ask to get outdoors to use a hole and the girls are complaining he eats too much to dump that amount." Johnny and strummed his mouth organ and the ape swung down from the RV roof and played on the mouth organ, 'The Last Mohican, 'so well Clay cried for being Nathan's side kick made him feel 'The Last True Alaskan Brave."

Where were his little braves in moccasins brandishing tomahawks and lances? There were none, his was a lonely job sacrificing family life to bring law and order to where cryptids lurked, and then there was the newspaper write ups and bonus cash rewards for using Mr. Sparkle tooth paste on the range, Mr. Sparkle underwear whitener, Dr. Ajax Midge repellent, Dr. Ajax rattler bite whitener paste to rub on the bite, so he got perks and cooking lessons from admirers.

"He was a much-loved lawman and comic writers were already using him as Tonto's nameless side kick to help the Lone Ranger fight lawlessness, giggle and an actor with big paps had already been lined up to play his part in a coming movie, wow.

*What is the actors name, no idea, **is a secret**."*

And since no horse did let the ape on the back as the ape did not know what toilet paper was for, Clay felt heartbroken watching the bow-legged critter carrying the water barrels, hen house for fresh eggs, and a shovel to dig holes quick, he bought the tricycle in Terlingua as they left, and the ape took to it quick.

"A hundred bucks' son," the shop keeper whose wife stood behind him holding a Winchester rifle pointed at Clay's important parts to have little braves. "This is a new emporium, the last one some idiot in an RV demolished and set on fire," the ship keeper in his striped apron with a handheld out.

Yes Sir, the Winchester was business Texas style.

Clay knew he was being ripped off, the bike was third hand and fire smudged and used in a circus by the dwarf bear to ride through burning hoops before the dwarf bear mugged the cashier and fled buying tickets on an Amtrak train heading to Yellowstone Park, see they often dressed the bear up as Charlie chapman so the bear sat in the train reading a Time magazine upside down, and yes, he had that little moustache and cane to whack the day lights out of the too curious.

Anyway, the ape sagged, wiped his brow, went to the water trough, and found it empty and looked at Clay.

"Tell you what, a hundred and will throw in the caramel cold drink and an ice cream peanut chocolate bar," the shop keeper as the Winchester cocked.

"Deal," and "Charge it to the town council," and that is when the Winchester went off. Chelsea might be the Council but there were council members, and the shopkeeper was one.

As another bullet zinged by Clay dished out the hundred.

"Bullets are ten dollars apiece," the wife knowing they cost 10 cents each.

And the ape drank, was refreshed, burped mightily, let of a smell, and cycled off to join Nathan ahead at the top of High Street.

"And no one knew what the top or bottom was of High Street giggle."

And Clay looked back, and a mountain lion was in the rear of the baggage train and the way the cat ogled him made Clay nervous and remembered Chelsea at her new handy back door wrapping her herself about him to smooch, pulling his head back by the hair so he might need a wig after that, **but that was alright, Chelsea was making him bald.**

"Take the cat, the Cattle Association hunt anything that moves, like that ape on the tricycle, and pinched his moons devilishly so welts appeared, and a false fingernail was stuck in one, **but that was alright, it was Chelsea's.**

"I want to puke giggle."

Clay spellbound replied, "Nice putty cat **come with me.**"

"And the pet vulture Alfred and twanged a garter from nowhere at Clay so it pinged off his startled nose that smelt the smoothness of bathed female leg.

"Here pretty bird," Clay **mesmerized** and took the ugly bald bird, **but it was Chelsea's gift so was alright.**

And where were was the baggage train going, to hunt down the badmen and the Chupacabra that had moved county but still raided.

And upfront Nathan stopped so those behind stopped and

he dug out of his pockets something all hikers should have, a small compass so small he could not read the arrows, but he was not looking for that, so dug deeper and pulled out a fold down telescope, but dug deeper for what every hiker wants, and found Martha's map and looked at it so much knew where the rips and folds were and dug deeper.

Those behind looked on with curious excitement, what would Nathan produce that every camper in the wilds should have, the squashed loo roll, no, the acid tablets, needed after eating food cooked locally, no, boot polish that he was training the ape to use not eat, no, postcards of the girls that he quickly hid, no, and found what he was looking for, a nut chocolate bar to eat between meals, and ate it.

Explains why Nathan vamoosed for his life as bullets, rocks, kitchen knives and forks, horseshoes and bedtime fairy tale books thudded onto him and the Luck of THE Irish was with him and he was unharmed, and not a drop of Irish blood in him.

And as Nathan ran, he found another peanut chocolate bar and stopping ate slowly as the baggage train watched and the rocks, knives and forks fell short of the sheriff, and as he was being childish, many eyes watched him thinking him cute as a dancing Texan Pork Belly reformed chop.

What beings could see Nathan as food?

Hungry critters that are who.

Critters with long flesh shredding claws.

Bigger fangs to rip you asunder.

And little brains to think what to do with the leftovers.

The boys should have turned the other way at that sign, 'SKIN WALKER RANCH THIS WAY, LIFE OTHER WAY,' but it would not have mattered as some delinquent had shifted the sign about so much no one could remember which way the sign should be pointing, and since no one cared no one fixed it.

The first thing Nathan knew he was in trouble was seeing his companions pointing and waving, shouting, and jumping about, reaching for GUNS except for Granny Smith who reached for a picnic hamper and the mountain lion that remained next to Clay, but did hiss and show fangs and hissed more and to show it meant business ripped Clay's trouser up, and not a hair on Clays legs broken as the mountain lion loved Clay.

Even Granny Nanny produced a derringer from a garter as every Texas granny keeps one as grandpa cowboys are still young at heart.

Grandpa Smith threw a lucky horseshoe that brought no luck to Nathan, as said, he did not have the 'Luck of The Irish,' as had no Irish blood in him, so the lucky horseshoe was unlucky for him.

"All I did was to eat two chocolate bars," Nathan thinking war was coming to him.

It was not from his companions but the thingamabobs leaping down upon his back salivating like shapeshifters should.

"Eat him please," Rodeo King watching far out point where Jesse the new Badman King had sent him, and Rodeo King went as Jesse had forty badmen cocking their guns itching to fill Rodeo King with lead as revenge for all the mean stuff he did them, like not give them their share of the rustling loot.

A suicidal thing to do when you have all these badmen wanting to KILL YOU for that.

And at Rodeo King's feet, Dolly the Chupacabra, that had taken a liking to him, see even a badman can be loved by a demonic dog with mange and probably rabid. What else did love Rodeo King?

"A battery-operated monkey on a mantel piece banging drums till the battery died, giggle."

But the shape shifters did not eat Nathan as they thought Nathan the cutest thing ever, so ran away with him leaving his ten-gallon hat to be picked up by Clay with tears in his eyes, saying, "Goodbye friend, Native American Natives have nothing to do with shape shifters, it was nice knowing you."

"You mean you are not going AFTER HIM AND RESCUE HIM?" Kung Fu Jackie at knee level.

"He was your best friend," Ragnar and after a silence trotted after Nathan.

For an instant Clay had a vision, not of Tonka but the girls all his, No Nathan Y fronts found in the kitchens of the girls, no Nathan rubber ducks in the girls bathrooms, no Nathan lollipops in the freezers of the girls, no spare ten-gallon hats in the girls cupboards, no Nathan hairs floating in his coffee made by the girls, no Nathan period as testerone shifted Clay's brain to his bottom where men think best.

And Clay's codpiece moved, yes, the brains were active.

"Murderer," Kung Fu shouted and followed Ragnar.

Now Tonka appeared to Clay, Tonka was not happy with Clay, Tonka did protect Clay against the shape shifters, Tonka did bless Clay with many girls' hero worshipping he could not count, Tonka did make sure Clay got a pay rise, Clay remembered a purple bra and middle fingers in the glass partition of a 4x4 instead as testerone filled his blood vessels.

Did Tonka really say all that in the split-second Tonka appeared to Clay?

And Clay span his colts and followed.

"Best friends s**t," he complained feeling he was the reincarnation of Custer.

The horses and pack animals did not follow, they had more sense.

The mountain lion did not follow either, human boyfriends were a dime a dozen so lay down next to Granny

Smith for the lion smelt freshly baked cakes.

Behind them Granny Nanny spread a picnic for her and Grandpa Smith to sit, use dainty fingers to hold the plastic cups, and napkins to wipe the cake crumbs away as they knew arthritic joints allowed them to watch, cheer encouragement and shield their eyes when a leg came overhead.

And shared the sugar cubes with the horses and pack animals.

Every now again opened a sardine tin and dumped the fish down the lion's throat.

*

"Now is our chance to steal men," Jesse not calling his gang 'boy' that was demeaning to badmen who ransacked your kitchen cupboards when you were at work, made a mess eating milk and cereals, did not empty the cat litter or take the dog out, left the television on, all the lights blazing and even napped in your beds so when you got home you of course screamed, "Whose been at my porridge, whose been wearing my slippers, whose been sleeping in my bed?"

And thinking your luck was in searched the house from loft to cellar for Goldilocks.

And the 'men 'followed Jesse to the baggage train.

"Neigh," they were greeted by those pesky horses that liked to run.

"Bray," the pack animals greeted them just waiting for these strange sweaty men to untie their reins from rocks.

"Look what I have found?" A badman looking forward to eating chocolate peanut bars that he emptied from Nathan's rucksack.

"These tastes fine," another badman chewing into mouthwatering 'chocolate bourbon pecan tart, a surprise for the lawmen and for Ragnar a chance to prove he was a chef.

"**This is better,**" another finding the bourbon that Ragnar tippled into his dishes to give them ZEST.

"**Look what I found,**" another badman holding up purple frillies exposing **someone's secret** and which of our boys' wears frillies under their riding chaps and foul chili breathes.

"Not Clay as I love him and he is a man, handsome, tall, tanned and wears colts to shot oh I love you Clay, not you Fili Pek, get away from me."

"The jackpot," another emptying a sack of bourbon plastic bottles so they would not clink **so the secret tippler** would not be discovered.

"My Clay would never drink as he took his job seriously and the only thing, he was addicted to was me, Fili Pek thought I told you to get lost, help."

And what is Fili Pek doing to Betty Lou that makes her flee for Spirit, **that is a secret** but here is a hint, he is playing at being a ghost dog.

"Look we are rich," another badman emptying Ragnar's silver and gold cutlery out, cutlery Ragnar produced when they had guests and since they never had guests the boys kept eating with their fingers, wiping their mouths with gloves, and the greasy gloves on their riding chaps, they were Texan men of the range for this mission, and being good lawmen took their Texan roles seriously so as to know their prey.

"Magazines, not cutting these up into squares for the latrine," and the boozy badmen ogled someone's private collection, and I know for a fact Clay would never buy such magazines so **who was the magazine collector** amongst the train?

"A mobile gaming app," and the drunk wiped out all the saved games on it, someone who stayed up nights playing these games, someone who played them on horseback, someone who spent all day in the outhouse playing these games **did be murderously mad.**

I know it was not Clay, he had a job to do awake.

And the badmen cheered for Jesse and blazed away into the sky and what goes up comes down.

Ahead a lone badman with Dolly wrapped about his feet looked back, now was his chance, he took out his Sharps Buffalo Rifle, aimed at what he thought was Jesse and fired.

Forty missed shots later he fired his last shell at what he thought was Jesse.

Who was this terrible shot? I know, do you? Who does Dolly that blood sucking creature love?

Where was Jesse? *That is a secret*, here is a hint, would you stay put watching forty badmen drop like flies because someone was shooting at you **and he knew who, do you?**

So, who shot the forty badmen? Here is a hint, what goes up comes down.

And what happened to Granny Nanny and Grandpa Smith, they sat there drinking tea and eating cakes, even offering some to the forty badmen who, "Thank you, you remind me of my sweet old granny," and "grandad you are spitting image of my grandad whom I never visit and missed his passing," or "these cakes are made just like my granny made them before I murdered her," and "Grandpa you can shoe the forty horses or start digging," Jesse meaning a shallow unmarked grave.

And being drunk the forty badmen saw three no forty mountain lions sitting about Granny Nanny and Grandpa Smith so did not rob these two as that is a lion per badman.

"Another time amigos," the badmen said to the forty lions and staggered away.

And just as Clay was closing the gap on the shape shifters, he was distracted by all the gunfire so being human stopped and looked.

"Clay I am too young to die, save me," a weak voice from a best friend or ex best friend as Clay saw purple frillies waved and remembered his time in the back of a 4x4 and Nathan at the glass partition waving a purple bra and giving him a middle finger.

Has Clay not awoken to the fact that it was jealousy making him hallucinate?

WE ARE ALL THE SONS OF CAIN.

And Ragnar stopped beside him and looked back and saw his bourbon drunk.

His chocolate bourbon pecan tart for desert eaten.

Tins of refried beans opened with toughened fingernails and poured down gaping mouths.

And Ragnar hoped the eaters choked.

But they did not as were blazing into the sky and ogling those private magazines and the owners of them narrowed his eyes and did not admit they were his, he did not want a bad name such as that 'Rollie Polly' overweight sheriff got, 'Watch out, he steals frillies from washing lines.'

And they looked at Ragnar asking silently, "Why do we eat with fingers?"

And the secret gamer was silent as he did not want to be called a Geek because he rode the range a Texan cowboy, lassoing cows, sucking rattler bites from another moons, as that is when the rattler sneaks up when you are defenseless reading a magazine and bites the exposed moon.

And because Nathan was being tossed from shape shifter to shape shifter in a game called, 'Catch the Piggy and if you miss you are out and the last one remaining gets first bite out of Nathan, so he never saw his chocolate peanut bars eaten so never went bananas.

Who would save Nathan?

"With Nathan eaten out of the Betty Lou Murders tales, did that mean my handsome Clay did be promoted sheriff, 'Sheriff Clay,' yes it had a nice ring to it giggle."

Update Ragnar from Iceland

Whenever I get the chance and a holiday from cooking, I go exploring for dinosaur bones for my PhD.

Trouble is I never get a holiday and Iceland is a far Away land where elves still live, sea monsters swim the seas, active volcanoes fill the sky with pumice, the arable land very little so we Icelander eat fish.

Our language is not real Danish as Celts on the west coast married their Viking blonde blued eyed opposites and Icelandic is a corruption of Gaelic and Danish and is so hard to speak, everything written about dinosaurs is in English, no wonder I immigrated.

I wanted to be famous by writing the first dinosaur PhD in Icelandic.

Now I want to open a world class restaurant in Houston and be a television chef, stuff dinosaur hunting amongst rattlers, thirst, and poverty.

And I am seething my bourbon I keep for cooking is drank. Am I the secret tippler, that would be telling.

Is that my magazine collection cut into squares for the outhouse, that would be telling also, but the ape can use them to be house trained.

I will suggest to Kung Fu he show the ape what to do so the ape copies him and where is that ape?

CHAPTER 10 WHO SAVES WHO?

Mouth organ music played badly could be heard as an ape on a tricycle rode past Clay and the others.

An RV was also heard coming towards them fast and decent mouth organ music heard.

And horses and pack animals as those horses convinced the badmen horses to ride away and not have to have another badman with silver spurs kick your ribs, whip you with a whip and for what, to sell you as glue and not a word of thanks or a retirement green field?

And a figure, a man was running behind them with bowlegs and cowboy boots not made for running, he should have carried spare trainers, but he did not for his name was, have you guessed?

He knew being out here without a horse was a lynching and intended to go amongst the train blazing and past them till he got his horse back.

So, is this badman a survivor of the shot up forty badmen,

or is it Rodeo King or is it Jesse?

And who shot up the forty badmen, remember what goes up comes down and not a lead bullet hit Granny Nanny or Grandpa Smith who drank their tea elegantly and wiped their mouths of cake crumbs and the lion slept peacefully next to them.

"My all this excitement has made me you know what Grandpa Smith?"

And Grandpa Smith grinned nodding and the two vanished somewhere for forty winks as oldies need a rest.

And Rodeo King mounted his horse and galloped after the running man blazing away and missed for, he WAS A TERRIBLE SHOT.

So, the running badman had to be a survivor of the forty badmen shot up or Jesse, read on to end the suspense.

"Best friend save me, I am too young to die, give Madam Wendy Lou my gold platted tranquillizer pistols, Cindy Lou my silver plate Yogi bear cod piece, Martha my piggy bank buried under our wood cabin in Alaska, Chelsea my collection of ten galloon sheriff hats and real silver badges," and he was asking his best friend Clay Eagle who started remembering his time spent in the back of a 4x4 and his friend ahead giving him a middle finger and waving a purple bra at him, "BUT CLAY HONEY, YOU WERE HALLUICINATING OUT OF JEALOUSY," but this time Nathan had committed suicide, was the shrimp insane, Clay was his rival in affection towards the girls, who cared about someone else, someone who played as mouth organ and had a better chest that Austin Powers, so wonder Johnny Christy had so many loves.

And the shapeshifters threw Sheriff Nathan yonder and the last was about to catch him, then clear of to eat Nathan up in privacy and not share a single bone with the other shapeshifters.

"Now where have we encountered greed before, think it was with forty badmen and Rodeo King who kept the loot to himself, oh well history has a way of repeating, giggle."

"Slurp," the shapeshifter licking Nathan so grass, grubs, and pooh particles as the wolf in the shapeshifter was strong and a wolf is a hairy dog and dogs lick their bums.

So, Nathan knew life without a best friend was lonely and perilous.

Then the sound of a tricycle and a sweating puffing out of shape ape and out of shape as usually sat on top of the RV making faces at passing folk who screamed, "A Big Foot, no one will believe me I saw one," then faint.

And it is a secret that the ape and tricycle flew over Clay and the shapeshifters and the one licking Nathan, and all were amazed at this circus act and applauded as the ape and tricycle disappeared over a cliff and were squashed a thousand feet below and out of the tale thank goodness.

No way, there was a splash and all sighed relief, the ape was ok, maybe not the bike.

"Now is my chance to escape," Nathan and ran the wrong way and disappeared over that same cliff.

Now was the time the lion was to go greet Clay as if nothing had got in the way of their relationship.

"Bye friend," Clay calming down becoming human again but not for long as a herd of horses and pack animals thundered over him.

Then that bow legged Mannie with blisters ran over him, so his spurs did nasty stuff to the deputy and thankfully missed the important places.

And Jesse exhausted and in pain from blistering feet got sweat in his eyes and wiped them on the run with his disease-ridden sweaty banana so his eyes smarted and he screamed, "Where is the ground under my feet," as he sailed over the cliff, never mind there were soft landings below.

Which would Jesse land on? Maybe bounce off one and then onto the other as a double act?

And Clay and all the others stood still watching the horses come back chased by a Chupacabra and Rodeo King blazing away with colts that never needed reloaded just like the movies, and how the film makers did that, only heaven knows because I do not.

And the horses and pack animals went over the cliff with all the recipes on 50 Texan dished and Ragnar shouted, "My booze," and ran after the pack animals, so HE WAS THE TIPPLER.

And skidded on horse mess and slipped over the cliff.

And Rodeo King seeing he was amid hungry shape shifters crunched AND was ready to draw on them when a Dire Wolf supposed to be extinct for thousands of years landed on him, flattening him, and ran off with him to eat him in private and not share a scrap of Rodeo King with his friends the shapeshifters.

And Rodeo King poked the Dire Wolf places, and kicked other places so the Dire Wolf was not concentrating and lept over the cliff.

"I am too young to die best friend, where the hell are you?" Clay heard Nathan below.

"Best Friend Chef I must save you to be taught the rest of the 50 Texan dishes for I AM A MARTIAL ARTS EXPERT AND FEAR NOTHING," SOUNDS LIKE AN IDIOT AND Kung Fu Jackie ran screaming BANZI and disappeared over the cliff.

No all this best friend c**p was getting to Clay, tears were forming in his eyes from all the dust kicked up.

Then the RV horns blaring came to a stop, a big rubber tire on Clay's left toes so explains why Clay was making funny FACES and trying to pull his foot free.

And the shapeshifters looked on amazed the circus had come to them.

And Madam Wendy Lou threw open the RV door, so it hit and bounced several times of Clay.

"Nathan loves I am coming," and she ran with a rope ladder and was so long she tripped on it and with these exact words went over the cliff, "Maybe Nathan you are not worth dying for, Johnny saves me, hurry,"

"Ha, that will teach her, thinks she is more pretty than me," and Cindy Lou full of jealously threw the RV door open again and strode to the cliff edge, and although she meant what she said, unplugged a rubber duck and with much hissing tossed it down to Madam Wendy Lou, but there were so many bodies down there, which was Wendy?

Then an inflatable fire escape flew over her, caught her pearl necklace so it broke, and pearls scattered and the inflatable fold down fire escape took her with her.

"Mm, that was not supposed to happen," and banjo strings strummed 1quickly adding atmosphere as Johnny Christy pushed the RV door open, so it bounced many times off Clay.

"Oh, hello Clay, just you and me and the shapeshifters, not to worry this is Skin Walker ranch and full of government agents, see I just press this button on my mobile and look, helicopters, 4x4's racing towards us, my friends are coming to save you imbeciles," Johnny describing his companions correctly.

Except the government agents were blazing away Texan style, questions asked later as dead men do not talk or complain and the blazers go home satisfied a day's work down.

And Johnny Christy vanished, and Clay thought he saw a cactus walking but a lion did not like walking cacti so mauled the cacti to bits that screamed lots, "Stupid cat, get off."

And the shapeshifters knew pearls were valuable as their human part could spend them in Terlingua when they became human so ran to the cliff edge to scoop up the fallen pearls and knocked, pulled, shoved each other over the cliff edge.

"Clay, if you do not rescue me, we will no longer be best friends," Nathan hollered up.

"I got these and why I am being rescued first," Wendy Lou truthfully for friendship has red lines.

"Mine are bigger, he will come for me first," Cindy Lou.

"GHH6t," the ape who knew he was being rescued first.

"Tonka," Clay now seeing Tonka and seeing visions of the good times he and Nathan had and filled with a sudden happiness shouted, "Best friend I am coming," and

Fell flat on his face, let us face it he had bumps all over his head from that banging door a palmist could read his future from.

"Mm," were Clay's last words as he passed out so who did he think of saving first, Nathan, the girls, that ape, the chef as Clay got hungry, Kung Fu?

Who?

None, Clay was knocked out senseless, but the lion did come and lick his face and cats are very clean animals, always licking their bums and willy and claws so 'GOD KNOWS what Clay got infected with?"

Then the ropes dropped from the helicopter and men in black shinny down the ropes, dozens of them all with black glasses and them hats.

"Eek," was heard from bushes as Granny Nanny and Grandpa Smith emerged with men in black behind them.

Nathan and the circus looked up at the dozens of men in black looking down at him from the cliff top.

Expectation filled Nathan and the others; they were to be rescued.

Then the helicopters and 4x4's took off sirens blaring.

"What about us?" Cindy Lou asked shifting her appendages in a wet bra that was shrinking from a wash threatening to pop out stuff.

"Gona kills them all," Madam Wendy flicking off a shapeshifter on her wet elastics that felt soggy and horrid and smelt like a dog.

Then the Dire Wolf Shaked all the cold dog smelling wetness onto them making their day.

Then the shapeshifters Shaked also flinging mud, snapping turtles and water moccasins onto the girls who screamed a lot, you would too with slithering reptiles in your elastics and not a single bite.

Then the ape threw his broken tricycle onto them, so they said together, "Ape is for the zoo."

And at the top mouth organ music heard and looking up a ripped torn cacti that deflated and Johnny Christy stood out covered in band aid.

"Hold onto the horses tails girls," Johnny shouted and with disgust they did so as that is the end horse stuff is jetted out.

"Here horsy, look what I got," and showed them sugar lumps and just like that the girls were next to him.

"Our hero," they swooned trampling on Clay under their wet feet, so they left leeches on him that the lion ate as desert.

And the door of the RV slammed shut, the engine started up and the RV was off.

"What about me?" Nathan squeaked still below and beside him Rodeo King who wanted him dead and Jesse who wanted Rodeo King dead before he was dead.

And Rodeo King drew a Bowie knife to skin Nathan out of his wet clothes and that is when Dolly landed on him as the Chupacabra missed him.

"I am off," the first sensible thing Nathan said and scrambled up the cliff embankment that was not steep so all of them could have escaped the bottom any time.

"They were attention seekers giggle."

He was followed by Ragnar holding Nathan's breeches for a lift.

And Kung FU "Gee Up Boss," as he sat on Ragnar's shoulders the lazy man.

"Puff pant I need to diet, "Nathan not realizing he carried extra.

Below them two badmen faced each other to in a dual like Texan men do with colts.

But the shapeshifters had other ideas, they were fed up with all this human craziness and ran over Rodeo King and Jesse, leaping here, gassing there, biting there a place, generally messing the two badmen up so their senseless bodies floated away.

"Are there alligators in Texan rivers giggle? Not to worry Dolly sat on Rodeo King steering, oh what a lucky man to have Dolly as a pet?"

But Jesse was not so lucky, he did not have Dolly, so the current was taking him into Terlingua, Martha and a hanging tree.

Would the town folk at last get drunk and have a lynching and fight as they do in all Westerns, so forgetting to lynch Jesse who did be rescued by an overweight sheriff and face off against Rodeo King later in a western Texan duel of colts?

You got to keep reading to find that out or did be a secret.

And Clay at last awoke strapped to the back of a horse as Nathan led the way back to Terlingua, a lion licked his mouth again.

They had got rid of the forty badmen who trailed behind roped quite dead, why behind, well this is Texas and gets hot daytime.

"We will be heroes best friend Clay when the towns people see these forty badmen, the governor will send for us back in Houston and give us pensions, medals and more fame Clay," Nathan dreamed.

And an ape was amongst the forty deceased badmen seeing what boots fitted him, what underwear, denims, Stetson hats, and strapped on colts, this ape was becoming intelligent.

In his checkered shirt cheroots, lighter, a packet of condoms he thought was a packet of chewing gum and was right now chewing and blowing one into as giant bubble.

In the back pockets are pictures of the forty badmen girlfriends, girlfriends if you had money to spend in Chelsea's or Purple Haze.

Dollars was dollars and the ape had stuffed much of these under his ten-gallon hat.

Why he just looked like a Texan who been online watching cows for six months, unshaven, smelly, thirsty, and lonely and full of a six month pay packet to get lifted by the girls at Chelsea's and the Purple haze.

"Oh well, they were in for a shock, yes apes were becoming human by associating with humans' giggle but not my Fili Pek, he is not human, he is a central European ghost for starters whose English is rubbish and keeps pretending he is a dog to get near me, he gives me the creeps because he is a creep, go away Fili Pek.

Tea break time, Granny Smith produced her picnic basket that never emptied of tea, cakes, and sardines. Granny had bought it from another elderly lady, Granny McPhee giggle."

*

Update Kung FU Jackie.

"I saw all the Bruce Lee and Jackie Chan films by the age of ten and had my first Dan, black belt by eleven.

I was the terror of every martial arts school, no one could defeat me, Jackie. Trouble it causes as I lined myself up for martial art films stopping others getting the part.

Film Directors saw me as a sassy kid who really BEAT THE DASYLIGHTS out of extras as I was Kung Fu Jackie and at thirteen wanted to impress the girls, knew girls wanted a tough man as a boyfriend so started BEATING THE DAYLIGHTS out of the film Directors to get my hundreds of admiring girlfriends film parts.

And one day awoke in a wooden box with holes drilled in the sides.

Holes that let in sea water as well as air.

I had been drugged and Shanghaied.

Fins circled me.

I swore I did repent my wrongs if Buddha did give me another chance away from the circling fins and I did be a humble dishwasher not silly film star, and guess what, the box was washed up on a Texan beach.

I was saved and answered Ragnar's advertisement for a dishwasher to go on journeys of adventure and action.

On the lonely prairie away from hundreds of girlfriends to help me break my promise to Buddha.

And now I am on the lonely prairie wanting back to Terlingua, who will save us from the shapeshifters and Dire Wolfs?

So, nobody saved this lot.

Who wanted to except one cowboy?

Update Kit

His name was Kit that was who and thought he did impress Martha by rescuing these out of towners. He was fast on the draw, a match for Rodeo King and Jesse.

He was a sideline in this story and is being brought in to replace the forty badmen who 'cashed their chips.'

He was good looking, tall but not dark and handsome like the tea leaves said, so Martha ignored him.

She really ignored him and life because Granny Nanny put Martha to sleep nights with an XXX laced hot toddy so Grandpa Smith *could sneak in to eat instant noodles with Nanny.*

So, when Kit tried singing Texan songs at Martha's window. She heard nothing.

A dejected spurned would-be lover is a dangerous man to himself and others. He span his loaded colts looking across the prairie for Rodeo King to fill with lead and take him back to Martha's, surely then she did notice him.

And he took a swig from a plastic bottle he had found on the prairie and was following a trail of plastic bottles cast aside by forty deceased badmen.

Kit was boozy.

He was drunk and could not care if he lived or died, Martha did not love him.

HE WAS WRONG.

Martha no longer had Granny Nanny or Grandpa Smith to make sure she slept nights.

Now she kept in a chest pocket over her right giant whatever, as big as that famous western singer, his photo.

His absence was making Martha long for him.

Sober up Kit and ride home, Martha needs you to do the ranch books, the tax forms, shoe the horses, brand some cows, and move into a spare room in her castle, and leave a string from your room to the front door or you will be like what some visiting tourists swear they heard, "Help, we are lost Japanese tourists," and "Give us food and water, we are done easting wallpaper and chewing carpets, we are German tourists."

And Martha was as good a businesswoman as Chelsea as thanks to magazines people came and paid to have a look about.

And you did pay also after travelling across the U.S.A. to visit, needing a latrine, Texan grub, am animated bronco cow in the yard that took any currency.

Yes, Kit was drunk and blazing away at anything moving.

The condor come up from Mexico whistling 'El Condor' and missed as he was drunk.

The coyotes toppling over as licked the insides of the plastic bottles clean and Kit thought he shot them all, nope, missed, the coyotes were as drunk as him.

The passing Comanche Indians out of the reservation for the day heading to Martha's to pose for photographs as they pretended to scalp Asian tourists from Bangalore.

Just as well Kit missed or they did peg him out and let that condor whistling 'El Condor' eat him all up, and who did know out here on the prairie?

They did know, not Tonka, Nathan and the rest coming their way waving for help as they were lost.

CHAPTER 11 A GOLF COURSE RUINED.

"Those are Native Americans, are we in a time warp Clay, go speak to them and see what they want?" Nathan encouraging his deputy pulling rank.

"They did scalp me for working for a white man," Clay and threw Ragnar out as he was small.

"No one does that to my friend," and Clay threw Jackie out also.

Both small men looked up the painted horse legs to the painted faces looking down at them.

One of the braves did a scalp motion showing the two men their fate.

"Chef I love you," Jackie hugged Ragnar and kissed him to

bits thinking they were to die.

"Get off, scalp me please," Ragnar holding his chef pants up as Jackie was accidentally pushing them down exposing a 'Tiger Lilly' cod piece, pink.

"Saw a film 'Cowboy or something about gay cowboys," Clay as the retinue watched Jackie push Ragnar flat.

Even the Comanche were amused thinking they were taking part in an adult film and looked about hoping for cash.

Then something amazing happened, Jackie pulled off a wig and face mask and BEHOLD, Jackie was a GIRL.

"You will not drink again or look at magazines, understood," and to emphasize 'understood' gave the Comanche a demonstration in martial arts.

"Groan," escaped Ragnar.

One of the Comanche rode up to the lawmen and said, "Smell you three miles away," pointing at the trailing badmen, and it was explained to them what happened.

A smile lit the Comanche faces, these idiots had survived meeting the shape shifters, they must be blessed by Tonka.

They did help take the lawmen back to Terlingua but first they were needed on a golf course as some President was having a birthday party for his daughter and wanted a wild west show for her.

The lawmen did have to follow, at least they did be safe.

Question was, would the Comanche and president be safe from our lawmen.

*

"Hole in one, I am the Greatest," the ex-President of the U.S.A.

"Oh, Great One, where is your ball?" The Governor of Texas practicing groveling.

"That cowboy on the tricycle swallowed it," the caddie, a

girl in flimsy attire for the sun was out and from well planted gardens a chorus of barber shop singers repeated, "The cowboy ate it."

Then cheer leaders somersaulted across the putting green.

"I want him deported, no true Texan would spoil my game," the ex-president being a member of the Rifle Club assembled a hunting rifle from his clubs.

Even the alligators in the pond dug to trap golf balls went silent.

The cheer leaders somersaulted in the air froze, how, gravity froze, how, ask Johnny Christy, he knows all such things.

The ex-President just had to ogle so shot a Comanche off his horse.

"Hehe," is Comanche for WAR.

The cheer leaders fell about the ex-president, one flooring him, saving him as a Comanche rubber tomahawk descended on him.

The governor of Texas being a Texan jumped on the horse the Comanche was riding with a "Yippee yahoo," and then focused on the name tag on the back of the Comanche Indian, **"Disney Indian, do not feed."**

By the time he had read the tag, the Indians had stopped at the back handy door of the golf mansion.

All about the mansion were manicured grass lawns, snake free for golfers, and electric golf carts and beyond the grass, Texas red dirt and long horn cattle.

"Happy Birthday to you," the Comanche braves sang as they were the hired staff for the ex-Presidents daughter.

"Oh, I feel faint," the daughter swooning pretending the braves were to kidnap, ravage her and turn her into a pregnant squaw.

"I will save you," and her millionaire boyfriend leaped from a verandah onto a magnificent white horse blazing into the air colts.

The Comanche were not worried, they know what happens when a stupid Texan man jumps from twenty feet up onto a hard saddle.

"Oh," the boy friend squeaked and fell to the dirt "Ohing."

That is when the **cowboy on the tricycle appeared**, scooped her up and vanished too where?

Ask the ape, as no one was looking for men in black who appeared with bazookas, flame throwers, a tank, two helicopters and many ferocious dogs.

"Howie, I am Sheriff Nathan Bottom, and this is my Deputy, Clay Eagle," Nathan.

And a golf cart stopped beside them.

A big man with fading blonde hair scrambled to get out of the electric golf caddie.

He looked about and at the dust cloud the cowboy on the tricycle was leaving.

"He is heading for Alaska," Clay said looking also.

"Wow," the Comanche braves impressed.

"Where is that smell coming from?" The president holding fingers to his nose.

"$10,000 each and there are forty of them, pay up and you can have them," Nathan and the Comanches knew how to count.

"Hehe," the Comanche which translated means WAR and will pay the hospital bill for the brave you shot in the moon, and they stole the forty rotten badmen who really were rotten these days, phew.

"Clay, tell them in Comanche I am the law and will hunt them down to Xmas to get my bounty back," Nathan prancing on his ten-gallon hat much peeved.

"Boss good friend, when did I ever speak Comanche?" Clay resigned to losing out again.

"I will give each of you a million dollars to bring my daughter back to me," and added, "of course not with twins."

"We are with them," Jackie being Asian knew a good business deal on offer.

"I just cook French cuisine for them on the range," Ragnar who cooked Texan grub but wanted a fresh start in life, in the air-conditioned kitchens of the president, and maybe a divorce.

"Wait a moment, he and Jackie were not married, oh just friends I see wink giggle."

"I am an old nanny and for a million will look after the girls twin papoose and to keep my mouth shut," Granny Nanny and the president clicked a finger and men in black dragged her away, so her trainers left a trail to a black van with antennae on the roof with a 'Disability badge' on the driver's window.

There were no license plates, **these were men in black.**

"I am not with her," Grandpa Smith swallowing edging away from the president.

"That is right, give RAGNAR IDEAS you miserable louse, that is your woman in the back of that van, can you not hear her laughing as they give her electric shot treatment to find out who she is?" Jackie sticking up for women worldwide.

And the governor of Texas clicked a finger and ten men riding gold horses all in white but with black glasses on rode up to Grandpa Smith and with lasso dragged him away to a tall tree.

"I am impressed, Texas style governor?" The president asked.

"Have a bourbon and a cigar president and let us watch the Texan show," and the caddie who could double as a cheer leader produced two-fold down chairs.

One of the cowboys pressed knobs on his phone and a lynching rope descended from the tree.

Grandpa Smith c***ed his breeks.

"I am the real law here, I am Sheriff Nathan Bottom, and I am taking that blacksmith back to Terlingua for trial," and Nathan span his gold-plated tranquilizer guns.

"There go our millions," Clay sadly.

"Terlingua?" Both political men and because they laughed so did the men in black and white cowboys with dark glasses.

"Ruddy?" Translated from Comanche means Terlingua and laughed then rode away in the direction of Terlingua for The World Hot Chili festival, where they did eat hot chili and not be able to ride a horse for a week, and being in fancy dress would blend into the Terlingua Festival of the dead and virtually stay in Terlingua all year for the many festivals getting money from tourists.

"Ruddy," the Comanche and thundered away.

"Here have a cigar boy," the president stubbing out a cigar on Nathan's head mistaking him for a mobile cigar ash tray.

Nathan fired the tranquilizer from his reaction to third degree burns on his scalp.

The President swayed and walked away gibberish.

The governor of Texas went after him, so did all the men in black and white Texans with dark glasses.

Clay picked up Nathan spitting on the smoking bit and went to rescue Granny Nanny as the black van driver's door had been left open.

Throwing Nathan headfirst in, he climbed aboard, there was Granny Nanny watching 'Tom and Jerry' reruns to obtain information from her.

Starting the engine, the laughing vehicle crashed into the lynching tree that sparked and smoked then burst into flame.

Grandpa Smith even with hands tied climbed aboard but Clay had crashed the van.

Steam escaped the radiator.

But they were lawmen of the old west and whistling many times for the horses were thick or deaf, the horses eventually came as Clay threw sugar cubes about.

"Get on all, ride them Yippee yahoo back to Terlingua and a million dollars for I know where that ape is going, to Highway 20 and hitch a lift back to Alaska," Clay tied Nathan on his horse, the other two did not need telling, they were off leaving a trail of lucky horseshoes.

Outside the mansion Ragnar waved goodbye, he was going to cook European elegant cuisine, but the president had his favorite chefs, but he did need a dishwasher to help the sixty others dish washers, all chefs who had hoped to cook for royalty.

"I divorce you creep," Jackie and ran and somersaulted trapeze style onto the back of Nathan where she sat on his shoulders viewing the horizon for an ape and a million dollars.

"There is the chimp," and pointed.

A mountain lion hiding at the nineteenth hole because Texan Politicians were Big Game Hunters roared and on two legs stood and beat its chest with taloned paws so doubled up.

Never mind it did give chase and not end up stuffed as a Stetson holder and paws outstretched for hats and mouth to take cigar butts.

And on a tricycle a young girl was able to peer closer at her abductor and screamed.

There was a Big Foot riding the bicycle not a cowboy.

"Help," she shouted.

Her rescuers on galloping horses and a pack train heard and were encouraged.

The trail was easy to follow, empty XXX plastic bottle the ape had stolen from Ragnar and banana skins.

Who would save the president's daughter and earn a million dollars.

The mountain lion, what would the lion do with a million dollars, why have Clay build an enclosed pasture for her to sunbathe in, a swimming pool to skimp in, and an unending supply of steaks.

This lion had become humanized.

Update Shape shifter

The shape shifter is a mean thing, tall, hairy, furry with long arms that end in talons to shred unbelievers as only unbelievers did be foolish enough to come to 'Skin Walker Ranch.'

Never mind wherever the Native American lived, so did they. Deer Women of the plains to the well-known shifters of the Southwest and even Clay might be one, a Kushtaka, an otter man of Alaska, and would explain his nightly sneaking outs behind his best friend Nathan to take part in cooking lessons with a common girl friend who only ate French Fries and Double Cheeseburgers, *oh yeh, pull the other one.*

He was a changeling, an Otter man with incredible energy thus serving Cindy Lou and Madam Lou and devouring their meals unfit for human consumption, as they were having cooking lessons, but Clay was not all human so ate their gruel disguised as Alaskan Poached Salmon, therefore proving he was an Otterman, a werewolf type creature.

"Wow, and I wrote this rubbish, giggle!

Were wolf, were deer, were otter, were cobra, vampire, all nasty so cannot be my Clay."

CHAPTER 12 HIM AGAIN

Comanche

"Mm, with a save and bath and expensive Taylor made clothes, something could be done with this Big Foot," as the president's daughter imagined him the biggest at the dance and the other girls envious of well, his giant cod piece.

Yes, a bath was needed as Big Foot never learnt what toilet paper was for, never bathed so stunk as that smell was a trail for other Big Foot.

A trail of marriage Big Foot style.

"I did need to teach him Texan swear words, ride a horse and be quick on the draw and run as the Vice President, daddy kins did never allow him to run as president. Yes shave, the whole body," the president's daughter **having her brains knocked about on a tricycle** so was not thinking properly.

And squeezed the ape's biceps so squeaked with delight.

The ape responded with wicked censored thoughts.

Lucky the ape was riding hard to get to Alaska or the silly girl did soon be having triplets all looking like daddy here and sent to a zoo with Ragnar to Iceland and far away as possible from elections, news coverage and dirt digging journalists.

Then the Cheshire grin on the ape dropped and he snarled so dirty yellow fangs flopped out, he was hearing mouth organ music.

"Yuck, definitely not kissing me till a dentist seen and teeth flossed, and you start using mint mouth wash regularly," the girl pinging a fang to see if it was rubber.

And the tricycle bounced off a gopher hole, so the girl's brains took a knock for the better.

The clouds of giant cod pieces shaped like never mind popped, she saw daddy kins writing into law 'HUNTING SEASON,' and she did want a skin on her guest room floor for when 'siss a secret' visited, they could roast waffles dripping runny chocolate in front of a log fire, and the glass eyes of Big Foot did smear with chocolate, so saw nothing.

Could not see anything, anyway, was skinned and a rug.

And the mouth organ music brought the gophers out of their borrows and they formed lines stretching back to the source of the mouth organ music.

A speeding RV.

The ape not to be out done played his own mouth organ, but badly as the gophers near him saw him and fled for their lives.

Then his front wheel buckled down a gopher hole that was not there a second ago.

"UJGFGH," translated means, "I am sailing."

And the president's daughter a trained cheer leader span through the air showing the ape the color of her elastics and why the ape was grinning as his head met Mr. Rock.

The president's daughter landed daintily on her feet and pulled down her dress, then calmly walked up to the senseless ape and poked him in both eyes saying, **"That is what you**

get for peeking bum."

And it was the sound of thundering horses and braying pack animals that alerted her to trouble.

"There she is and there He is again," Clay peeved his million-dollar reward was going to you know HIM.

But was it, something happened, this was America where dreams come true.

Suddenly an otter was leaping off the galloping horse running on two legs to the president's daughter.

"A monster, a were-wolf, no were-whatever is going to ravish me before eating me, I am off," and the president's daughter turned to run but Mr. Rock was in the way.

"Oh, my head hurts, oh what have they done to my ape, let me kiss you better," the president's daughter unhinged as bits of gangrene dinner hung from the apes' fangs so his breath stank.

Then he heavily winded so the president's daughter fainted, **heaven had pity for her**.

Then the RV stopped beside her, and a side door flew open catching a passing speeding Otterman full force so the were-creature poofed back into Clay Eagle, winded, brainless, and senseless.

His spinning eyeballs did manage to see Alaska Woman descend and Wonder Bra Woman also out of the RV. They both were in purple leotards, there had to be something missing with Clay if he only thought of women in purple lingerie, perhaps it was Him not that overweight sheriff stealing purple bras from washing lines.

"Oh, what am I thinking off, my Clay likes purple, I am wearing translucent purple elastics, Fili Pek are you in purple Y fronts, see, Clay is normal, giggle. Mm, Fili Pek is wearing purple frillies not Y fronts, get away from me, bad dog Fili Pek."

But none had a plan B.

Kit arrived with a sore head, was he the Plan B?

A mountain lion no longer loved Clay; it was in love with Otterman.

"Whoa horse I said Whoa," as Nathan arrived and as his horse abruptly stopped, he **sailed away out of the tale.**

And Kung Fu Jackie saw her million dollars vanishing in layers of wonder woman knickers so went bananas.

"Ha so," Jackie as she spang towards the wonder women who of course side stepped, and Kung Fu Jackie **sailed out of the tale** somewhere with Nathan.

"I am pretending to shoe this mule," Grandpa Smith peering, no, he was ogling purple stockings, so Granny Nanny went bananas and beat him senseless.

Well, that takes care of the lawmen.

And the wonder girls unraveled a purple carpet fit for emperors and a line of battery-operated monkeys playing cymbals were thrown out the RV door to line the carpets edge and provide musical atmosphere.

Yes, atmosphere so the tension built up, the wonder women felt it so great they wanted to dribble, and Johnny Christy leapt out of the RV all in black, yes with the glasses.

A gold pistol in a holster.

A chest so hairy the red hairs pushed upwards up Johnny's nose.

And the Egyptian mummy walking reached the president's daughter.

"I will take this back ape," Johnny as he snatched back the ape's mouth organ.

Although senseless the ape managed a TEAR.

That is when the president's daughter punched Johnny somewhere, so he groaned and rolled away out of the tale.

"Never mind darling, I will get daddy kins to buy you a gold mouth organ," and the ape smiled.

Who saved the president's daughter and got a million dollars?

Was Kit just arriving with a hangover.

The president's daughter looked up, the Texan suns dazzling her brain senses, so she saw a young handsome man on a horse. At first, she thought it was her boyfriend come to rescue her, but she knew he was in a wheelchair and useless after dropping twenty feet onto a hard saddle.

And she looked at the ape, a monster, not human, yes, she was human again, and tossed the ape's head aside to meet Mr. Rock again.

Kit did not even ask her on his horse, only he was aware of a girl leaping in the air completing geometrical shapes flashing her elastics and white socks.

Martha never treated him kindly like this girl but there was a problem with Mr. Kit. Had he met Mr. Rock earlier that we did not know off?

Even the knees and white trainers failed to stimulate Kit, his brain ached, his breath smelt of **stale XXX**. He needed a shave and had drunkenly peed in the saddle as his MAN Pad was full, **so stank**, had he done a number two, let us sniff?

And with shaky hands from too much XXX started rolling a roll your own.

"Has a naughty boy been out on the town then?" The president's daughter asking for trouble.

Kit looked about for a young naughty cowboy. That is when the president's daughter saw wrinkles, Kit was not young, why should he be, he was Martha's foreman with years of experience chasing long horn cows in the blazing dehydrating skin wrinkling sun, to freezing the b***s off in the snowstorms as Texan nights can be cold.

Same as Martha, both girls saw a wizened prune.

Shame.

But she did like his pearl handled colts in a black holster, this man was a gunfighter.

No, he was the wizened old foreman of Martha's looking forward to a retirement home for cowboys.

Little did he know Martha worked her boys right up to the entrance of the 'Pearly gate,' as she was some businesswoman.

"HGGHH," translated, "my million dollars," ape unsteady on his feet but knew a million dollars would, back in Alaska provide a centrally heated cave with a swimming pool where floozy Big Foot girls splashing about leaving whoopsie floating and discoloring the stale water yellow crawling with liver flukes.

"Apes just did not know where he was better off giggle."

"Girls are not all they are made out to be then?" Fili Pek adding at last an intellectual question.

"Oh yes we are," and he provided strange green colors in the atmosphere as I beat the LIVING DAYLIGHTS OUT OF HIM for even daring to think such thoughts.

For food the ape did have it delivered by students etching out a living.

But Mr. Rock had knocked his peanut sized brain to think human ways.

Then the Comanche raided and left.

"I am to be thrown into a tepee and married to a buck who smells of buffalo grease," the president's daughter with the Comanche.

Lances with rubber heads, arrows, tomahawks, all fake for Disney made littered the earth about the ape who gingerly felt for his important parts or there did never be any baby Gigantopithecus whose first words would be, "Hawg," translated means "give me food bum."

"Gr," the ape ripping apart his sweaty human clothes as he had been tricycling hard.

"Gr," as he held up the tricycle with a busted front wheel. That should teach him not to hurry.

"Gr," picking up Grandpa Smith as he was harmless and shook the smith so both brains rattled.

"Gr," the ape toned down having taken his annoyance out on Grandpa Smith who needed stitched up as Ape had bit, snarled, tore, and **breathed** on Grandpa Smith because the president's daughter was disappearing in the horizon with Comanche.

Not with him.

And the ape knew the Comanche did make fur saddles out of him to keep their moons warm for Texan nights are cold.

"What would the ape do now giggle?"

He was ogling the wonder women thus proving humans are descended from apes and males evolved from the contents of unwashed trash cans.

"Go after her ape," Alaskan Wonder Woman leaping and turning so she landed on apes' neck and twisted it, so he looked up into a masked face.

"Yuck, what you been eating," as pinged away a lizard eyeball from a fang, and the twisting hurt ape as he felt his neck bones creak **but that was alright**, apes had seen appendages close.

Then, "Go after her ape," as Wonder Bra Woman landed on his chest using his big ears as anchors. Her stilettos were making holes in the ape's chest, **but that was alright**, apes were getting a close-up view of appendages.

Apes was on his way to ape heaven.

Why, the girls wanted to show apes they were not his type and go eat a banana and not serious about him chasing the president's daughter.

"There were limits to the tale of 'Beauty and The Beast giggle.'

But that was alright as apes was getting close view of appendages and when the 'WONDER GIRLS' twigged to apes heavenly bliss, one beat him with a bra and stiletto shoe, and the other wanted to know how fast the ape could swivel his head 180 degrees a hundred times, **but that was alright**, apes were getting close views of appendages.

Then mouth organ music played and a man with a squeaky voice said, "Come on girls, time is a wasting, a million dollars is mine," Johnny and did not use the word OURS.

FOOL.

SO, an RV drove off without him.

Never mind he was Johnny Christy of Alaskan Fame and capable of anything.

Was he to unzip his 'Austin Power Hairy Chest' and produce an electric fold down bike and was that weight of the bike making him walk funny?

Would he produce a D.I.Y. aero plane kit strapped to his legs, and was that why he was walking funny?

Would he kick off the soles of his cowboy black boots and rev up **micro-engines** in his boot heels so he could run faster than a cheetah and was that why he was walking funny?

Would he wiggle his dark glasses so 007 lasers appeared with cross hairs to take down the departing Comanche and was that why he walked funny as the glasses were too dark?

Would he reach down to his moons with a lighter and ignite the gases there so he could fly like a rocket towards the Comanche or explode him to heaven and was it the internal gases making him walk funny?

Whatever he better hurry as the Comanche were disappearing over the Texan Pan Handle and so was the RV with his favorite cold caramel drinks in the fridge.

But they were there and he here getting thirsty under the hot sun.

And he walked funny to a hole the ape had dug earlier and left a trail of loo paper to, and here Johnny Christy became human and gave us the reason why he walked funny.

We had forgotten that when the president's daughter had her brains knocked about and was seeing the ape as a handsome suitor, she had punched hard an upper cut to an important place where Johnny kept his jewels.

And Johnny Christy used the ape's hole in the Texan Pan Handle to let rip all that gas he had in him.

"Argh," Johnny sighed.

"Bloated from drinking galloons of fizzy caramel drink daily that built up the gases."

And Johnny Christy became airborne as the gases shot him skywards and out of the story?

Update Comanche Braves

They knew they were the kings of Texan Pan Handle.

They rode their horses where they pleased so picnickers had to very careful were they spread the tablecloth.

They knew who they had with them, The President of Estonia's daughter and he did pay them a million US dollars to have her back in Far Away Fairy Tale Estonia.

In fact, they had another president's daughter, and this was because all these braves knew Estonia was not part of Texas but New York.

They were all going to meet Tonka soon.

With the million-dollar reward, they did build their own 'Comanche Roller Coaster Land', casinos, chicken farms, new settlements full of Comanche people. Cars banned; horses would make a comeback; the Amish did be welcome.

Loved by their people as totem poles in their likeness erected in the new settlements.

Of course, new settlements cost money to run, so they did tax the poor, good, wealthy, ugly and bad to stay in the million.

But these were Comanche descended from Comanche raiders that burned log cabins, rustled long horns, and fought John Wayne's army.

They knew what a million dollars did buy so dreamed of MEXICO, tequilas, floozy women, not squaws, Cadillac's that ran on petrol not horses you had to get up early and brush down and wash out their stables of manure.

Yes, these guys were going already using their mobile phones to arrange a meeting with the Men in Black to exchange this troublesome girl who kept asking, "When am I going to be thrown in the back of a tepee and eat buffalo jerky?"

She was driving them loco.

She just kept nattering.

She just kept squeezing your biceps.

She just kept looking places a decent girl should not.

She was the president's daughter and a spoilt brat.

And the braves ride into Terlingua celebrating 'The Dead Festival.'

And tourists took selfies.

The braves held out hands for dollars and keen eyes clicked they were real Comanche.

"Boys we got a lynching at last, "Martha not caring if this was The modern era, a Comanche was still a Comanche and they had not had a lynching in years.

Martha's men rallied to her command.

A few fell out from behind pink curtains full of perfume haze colts blazing.

Some ran out of the Purple Haze colts blazing but tripped up on their jeans and if the jeans were not at ankle level they did be safe.

Others crawled out of Chelsea's swivel doors colts blazing.

A few surfaced from water troughs guns blazing.

And the tourists thought it great, a fake gun fight with actors just for them, and the rubber arrow heads of the Comanche reinforced that notion.

Until the Terlingua cottage hospital was full of a thousand shot up tourists.

"It was awesome, real bullets used, I will return next year," a scalped tourist.

And Martha thought of Kit, he never got drunk, he did have taken care of those Comanche with hands tied behind his back, yes, he was a Texan full of True Grit and she was a Texan girl who was full of **imagination.**

CHAPTER 13 THOSE SAILING RETURN.

Men in black

The Rio Grande had objects floating in it, those who had sailed out of this story and needed a splash to land safely in.

Amongst rip roaring rapids, giant boulders to be bashed to smithereens on, poisonous snakes getting a free ride to populate down steam urban gardens, circling fins, discarded inflatable shark toys, those in the sky splashed fearful as a waterproof radio floated by blaring, 'Sharkie dance.'

"Cur," a white rapid shooter, in other words a tourist who pays a local for a raft and a paddle and is never seen again as the raft is smithereens to bits on giant boulders.

"Cur," canoeists, tourists who paid local Comanche for the wooden dug outs that were so heavy they sank and?

"Awesome, better pick them up rangers," a park ranger of Big Bend Park.

Pick what up?

"A tall handsome wet deputy that needed stripped off and dried with a towel giggle."

"We are lawmen," Nathan began, and the park rangers gathered about him peering down at him. It was unfair, they were judging Nathan by his small stature, not capabilities.

"Neigh," and "bray," the equines that had clambered aboard tipping the raft upwards so Clay held onto Nathan and the rudder and the extras, the rangers were gone but cursing and splashing was heard as the Rio Grande sped them to the shallows at Terlingua were they wanted revenge, no, they wanted dry clothes as the wet underwear stuck places and the wet shirts glued arm to arm pit, and there were medicinal leeches needing taking care off.

And Grandpa Smith and Granny Nanny were absent.

The vulture given Clay by Chelsea?

The mountain lion looking for Otterman.

Where was that foolish Gigantopithecus?

And Mr. Kit.

Dolly that blood sucking vampire on four legs?

A pack of blood sucking Chupacabra?

Rodeo King and Jesse?

An overweight Sheriff?

Dire wolves.

Shape shifters?

Martha and Chelsea.

A speeding RV.

Wet park rangers.

Wet Rio Grande tourists.

A President playing golf.

The men in black?

The cowboy men in white-on-white horses with dark glasses?

A boyfriend who now walks funny.

Johnny Christy, still the best secret agent in the world, was 001.

Bet you did like to know there whereabouts, so did I as extras cost money and food to feed, a private company to empty the mobile latrines, well you cannot have them and all the Comanche, the revived forty badmen, cowhands and Terlingua citizens looking busy doing business anywhere, **what would happen to The Pan Handle?**

Where were these exciting characters, *read the next 10,000 pages to find out?*

*

Terlingua was quiet, all the tourists arrived for the Dead Festival were alive queuing at latrines as they had eaten a lot of chilies in The Terlingua Hot Chili Head competition, now needing to chill out and drink Chelsea's XXX listening to Country western Music, then Line dance at night and do what excited tourists do.

Exchange Game Playing cards of course and return to the latrines as that chili takes days to leave you.

And the Town Council grew rich as Chelsea rented the mobile latrines to the Town Council herself and the loo paper was not free, so the cash machines at Chelsea's were heard all hours.

And loud satisfied sighs from the latrines.

Why was Terlingua quiet and the streetlights, car lights, search lights, torches and light from glowing cheroots making daylight?

A pack of Chupacabra had run over the adobe roofs laughing and sucking the daylights out of rubber chickens as this is a non-violent tale, so all the tourists took mobile selfie snaps, while the citizens lit pitch forks to ward off the devil dogs, the overweight sheriff seen to climb the roofs shouting to the Chupacabra, **"It is me, take me to Rodeo King our Boss,"** and being overweight the drainpipe he was climbing up broke, slowly so he saw below a crowd so gulped.

And he fell too many hands that ran carrying him to the **'Hanging Tree,'** and why he had gulped.

Has the fool not confessed to who was the Boss of him and the devil dogs.

And Martha was in town, *"Tough luck Overweight corrupt Sheriff, to the lynching tree you go giggle."*

But he was overweight and the horse they sat him on sagged, the rope stretched, and he was now just able to touch the ground with his toes.

He better not need that mobile latrine.

And the reason why all the people were quiet was at one end of High Street was Rodeo King walking funny ready to draw.

At the other end of High Street Jesse also walking funny ready to draw.

On each other.

*There could only be one **King of The Badmen**."*

Anyway:

"I see Martha's in town, I am going to the jailhouse to dry out," Nathan quickly looking at Clay to see if he was believed, the front door was a handy exit when you were small and fast on the toes with the ten-gallon hat pulled down hard to hide the face.

"I see Chelsea's in town, I am going to the jail to dry out, and out the handy back of the jailhouse and run from trash can, to bush, to washing lines to Chelsea's and cooking lessons how to make soft cheese from non-existent dairy herds, would you believe?" Clay peeking at Nathan to see if his hook, line, and sinker been swallowed.

And their eyes met, narrowed, and looked the other way.

They had lied fibbing and supposed to be the best of friends too.

"He thinks I am going to Martha's but will make my way through the crowd to Chelsea's," Clay thinking so his brain hurt.

"If Clay thinks I am off to Martha's I am in luck for being fed by Chelsea soft cheese made the night before by her and playing 'Peek a Boo,' upstairs," Nathan wondering how Chelsea made the cheese without milk so his brain hurt?

Then remembered a 'SIMPSON EPISODE,' where the hoods sold milked rat milk to schools, and Nathan shuddered, would she, there were many tunnels leading from her illegal XXX brewing chamber that Nathan being a good lawman ignored as he was here to catch a rustler and end the Chupacabra menace.

Besides he liked Chelsea, and the reason why is a secret, and she was some businesswoman.

Yes, silence as the crowd waited for the badmen to draw on each other, and to their delight wet lawmen appeared to draw on the badmen, and the question was now, would the badmen no longer draw on themselves but the lawmen.

Wait a minute, the lawmen were unarmed and squelching.

"Someone throws them guns," it just takes sone.

"Friend what are you doing at Chelsea's front windows?" Nathan acting innocent smelling the yellow roses of Texas.

"Friend, I see you like roses," Clay wanting an excuse because he was at Chelsea's front windows, and got one, "Chelsea is teaching me to make soft Greek cheese."

And Nathan knew who was making the soft cheese now.

And the lawmen drew apart to draw for only the survivor could win Chelsea.

But they were unarmed until it only takes one, "Someone throw them guns."

And Mouth organ music was heard behind the pink curtains of Chelsea's as she appeared at a window.

"Why hello boys, bye boys," and drew the curtains but went to another window to peek as had put bets on each duelist to win.

The lawmen looked at each other, once again Johnny Christy was before them, and they had fallen out over a woman.

"Forgive me Clay," Nathan hugging Clay's knees.

"Always best friend," Clay patting his boss's head.

Then the blazing started.

"Take that and that," Clay blazing his expensive colts.

"And this," Nathan firing a bazooka someone had thrown at him and the heat from the back set fire to the pink curtains.

"Whoops," Nathan ditching the bazooka for a Winchester.

And the blazing pink curtains were dragged out by Chelsea's staff, so Rodeo King thought of XXX as he was thirsty.

But Jesse being A LOW-DOWN skunk did not stop blazing away and ran up toto his old boss the one he used to love and blew Rodeo King to HELL.

"I loved you, but you hated me and kept beating the living daylights out of me," Jesse and wiped tears away, "now I am thirsty, where is all that cold caramel drink," and Jesse began to walk away, to the Purple Haze with his back to the prone Rodeo King who was doing a lot of leaking red stuff.

It was ketchup as all good cowboys keep a bottle in a breast pocket to cover the Chili Burgers in and that is how Texan manage to eat their chili, disguised, just like the advertisements **you get in the movies.**

And Rodeo king opened an eye and lifted his colt and aimed at Jesse's retreating head and pulled thew trigger.

The pistol was empty.

"The luck of the Irish is with Jesse," Rodeo King and shut his eyes.

And a hungry pet vulture fed up waiting to be fed flew done and carried Rodeo king aloft, then found him heavy, dropped him onto the adobe roof of the cottage hospital so he sprang a bit on the bed he landed on.

"Now that is the Luck of \the Irish giggle."

Surrounded by student doctors and nurses who were waiting for their first medical lessons, but the robotic paramedic Chelsea bought to save the Town Council hiring a real doctor was outside attending to them hit from the blazing guns.

"E.T.," just takes one and soon the robotic paramedic was whizzing and spinning smoking and came to a stop at Chelsea's feet who was fuming, someone was going to foot the bill as she was some businesswoman.

And we leave Rodeo King screaming in the capable hands of the hospital staff.

"Look we can lynch Jesse, he is skinny," it takes one and as Jesse had put his guns away, basking in his glory, dreaming of cold caramel drink and waitresses dressed as waiters, the crowd silently sneaked up behind.

"Mm," he managed as a handy chloroform bandana was put over his mouth and he was dragged by his boots to the lynching tree. **Just like the movies** as all good cowboys keep a bottle of chloroform in a breast pocket, why so many unruly cows at branding time, unruly bed bugs, unruly bank managers, unruly Chelsea girls, yes, a bottle comes in handy **just like the movies**.

And his boots came off.

"Mm, my size," someone in the crowd.

So, they dragged him by his shirt till all the buttons pinged off and with it an Austin Powers glue on red hairy chest.

"My cat needs a new bed," someone.

And the ripping off the hairy chest awoke Jesse who went

for his colts.

"Looking for these?" Someone.

So, they dragged Jesse to the lynching tree by his red Long johns that came away.

"For the bin," someone.

"Who is going to pull him by his TED cod piece?" Them all and as there were no volunteers dragged him Texan style to the lynching tree, with a rope about his neck.

And Martha watching on her tenth cheroot and 20th tipple from Chelsea's was seeing double KIT, so threw her cheroot away and the breeze blew in onto a rebuilt wooden front of an adobe house, so it went in the open window for the day was hot and set fire to the bedding.

Did anyone shout, "FIRE," and get buckets of water to put out the fire.

No, they were busy lynching Jesse.

Yes, Kit had just rode into town and saw his love, Martha.

A drunk Martha about to topple over.

And Kit rode over to her and looked down, he never been that close to her before, she was aging, wrinkles were under her eyes and that appendages, was that a rubber tube to inflate them, and her blonde hair was dyed, she was a red hair, and her fingernails were false, was that belly fat showing through her opened shirt. "What have I been in love with all, these years?" He asked as Martha pulled him off his tall horse and as she dragged him under a wooden planked pavement, The Luck of the Irish was not with Kit or Martha.

Underneath the wooden pavement planks are where the rats lived eating the dropped Texan Cowboy Stews and the rattlers that ate them.

Was this the end of Kit and Martha?

No, the pack of hungry Chupacabra sensing blood under the

floorboards and having long claws, ripped the planks off, the rats fled, the snakes went after the rats, and did the Chupacabra suck all the blood out of Kit and Martha, not all the scampering rats and slithering snakes got their hungry attention.

Now we could say the Luck of the Irish was with these two but as Martha smooched and struggled with the bronze buttons on Kit's denims, she was sick.

All over him.

She was drunk and drunks got sick.

Who was Kit to judge, was he not just getting over a hangover?

Now he needed to push Martha off him and get them both to a horse water trough.

But all that upper weight made Martha heavy, and she was sick again.

That gave Kit energy, and he dragged his love to a nearby horse water trough and threw Martha in, there was a thud, them thirsty Chupacabra had drunk it dry.

Just as well he knocked Martha senseless as she was not the type of cowgirl to take being roughed up quietly.

And Chelsea had pity looking at these two.

"Girls get the fire hose," and Chelsea did bill them Town Water Rates for she was some businesswoman.

"Hey, the town is on fire again," takes one, "bring that fire hose over here Chelsea," and the girl rubbed fingers together and her girls appeared with Winchesters.

She was some businesswoman.

Then the men in black arrived, why, well the president had arrived looking for his spoilt daughter.

"I was tempted to leave her with the Comanche, but her mother did beat the living daylights out of me," Mr. President and swung a golf club hitting a passing Chupacabra away from him.

"I will build a golf club in Terlingua and a private zoo to attract golfers to feed the Chupacabra peanuts, breadcrumbs, burger buns, chili burgers, ice cream cones so will build a takeaway providing more jobs.

Terlingua will one grateful and vote for me," Mr. President.

And a smart Chupacabra sat next to him licking the dust of his golfing shores.

"Hey boys look at this," Mr. President speaking to the men in black who surrounded him flame throwers pointed at the devil dog.

"Got a name doggie?" Mr. President.

"Dolly," the chupacabra replied and rolled over a few times playing dead, jumped a somersault and landed on its head so pretended it was senseless, then whined rubbing its belly.

"This one I will give to my daughter," Mr. President.

The flame throwers were put back on safety just as well or there did be no Mr. President.

So, Dolly found a home.

"Buys, we can glue an Austin Powers Chest on the mangy parts, give it a collar and a doghouse, and a bath straightaway, these Texan dogs sure do stink," Mr. President.

Yes, Dolly had evolved into a house dog.

A vampire dog that would suck the blood out of anything smaller in the neighborhood.

Is this why the President gave the walking mange to his daughter, she lived in a neighborhood where the opposition political party lived, was this a doggy murder, no, we are dealing with the president and his spoilt daughter.

"Four," The president sending a golf ball to hit Jesse in the back of the head.

"Is he dead?" A lyncher.

"Can we lynch a dead man?" Another.

"We are in Texas, we lynch anything that clucks," another.

"Did not hear him cluck," another so the lynchers moved away from Jesse about to be lynched next to the overweight corrupt sheriff.

And a leprechaun was seen ruffling the pairs pockets for coin, so the luck of the Irish was here after all, and a thieving Leprechaun.

And the leprechaun took Jesse's cod piece as with a wash in disinfectant he could wear it to impress the girl leprechauns back in green Ireland.

And just like a convoy of trucks, cement mixers, R.V.s, mobile chicken ranches, casinos, television stations, political party offices, toy shops, five-star hotels and cheap motels round the next adobe for never mind.

And the town burned down again.

"Saves demolition bills," Mr. President.

Then the Dire wolf ran amok, but not just one, a pack of them.

"I got to have them back north, the dogs back there are punny compared to these Texan German Shepards," Mr. President and "boys, get me them."

Men in black take their jobs seriously and catching aliens living amongst us disguised as porn magazine sellers to catching extinct Dire Wolfs was what they were paid for.

They were men in black and about to be shredded.

"What does the nation pay you for?" Mr. President complaining about the lack of progress in catching a single Dire Wolf.

"Catch them yourself," takes one and soon a pile of dark

glasses lay at Mr. Presidents golf shoes.

Not to worry, Dolly was growling protecting Mr. President.

It wanted its own supply of men in black and its own dark glasses as every vampire dog should have a pair if running about in daylight in Texas, and explains the RED SORE DRY eyes, some eye drops needed but who in their right mind would that close to a Chupacabra.

Then the shapeshifters arrived scaring the inhabitants of Terlingua stupid. Scaring the s**t out of them so ques formed at the mobile latrines and Chelsea smiled, she could hear the clink of a dollar to open the latrine.

The mayor needed a pay rise, she was the mayor, she was some businesswoman.

And LOOKED at Mr. President, it was time to introduce herself.

And many unemployed Terlinguans picked up the dropped dark glasses and formed a circle about Mr. President.

No dire wolves would get through them.

Did the new men in black get ripped to shreds.

No way, the dire wolves knew they were Texans full of True Grit and indigestible.

What about the shape shifters, they ran after the other men in black were helicopters waited to take them back to Skin Walker Ranch.

"Four," Mr. President knocking one out of a helicopter.

"It can do as a rug for the front foyer of my penthouse tower," the president. The man was lethal with a golf ball, who next on his list?

"I will take that," the voice of the law.

Mr. President looked about for the speaker.

"I said I will take that," the speaker again.

The President looked down at Nathan.

He focused on a ten-gallon hat with a badge pinned on it.

The president lifted the hat and saw Nathan and smiled "A true Texan with True grit indeed," Mr. President.

"We are Alaskans, and I am sheriff here so give me the golf club," Nathan obviously needing a holiday from law enforcement.

"He meant no harm," Clay picking Nathan up and about to vamoose.

"A real native American, well I am the son of a golfer," Mr. President remembering his favorite Lone Ranger Saturday matinee films.

Who would rescue our lawmen from a penal colony on the moon?

It was someone's daughter, and a war party of Comanche braves a whooping and hollering.

They rode up and down High Street a few times adding horse mess then stopped near Mr. President.

"She yours?" They asked.

"Daddy Kins it is me," someone's daughter.

Mr. President gritted his teeth, "she is back," he mumbled.

"A million dollars you promised, pay up Sir and then we can talk about the treaty you made with us back in1889," a Comanche brave going to the moon also.

"Listen Tonto, I was not born back then," and Mr. President blew a whistle.

A dog whistle only real men in black heard, them aboard helicopters who now covered their ears in pain.

There was only one-way to stop the whistling, go back to work.

"I will take this," and Nathan did, "I am Sheriff Nathan

bottom and this my Deputy Clay Eagle," and was to add "arresting you for jaywalking, but Clay with a laugh tossed Nathan aside and skimped away to join him.

Clay threw back the golf club.

There was a clunk as Clay sent Mr. President to the stars.

"Daddy kins," and the ferocious daughter tore the living daylights out of the Comanche brave holding her to go to 'daddy kins' aid.

"By Tonka just take her," and the braves cleared off.

"Charge," a man in black and takes one and they charged the Comanche and do not worry, the Comanche knew the flame throwers and submachine guns the men in black aimed at them were fake, a movie was being made.

"Fools giggle."

And a flying saucer appeared, had come down from Skin Walker Ranch and escorted by F-16s.

Today would be a day to remember, E.T. Day would be added to the celebrations Terlingua offered tourists.

The Battle of Comanche Pass for Native American buffs and re-enactment dress uppers.

The Day of The Dire Wolf Day where tourists could dress up in were-wolf costumes and pink undies if they wanted.

Cash was coming.

And Shape Shifter Day when for a week the real shape shifters visited allowing selfies and more cash to the Town council.

And the Gun Fight at the Terlingua Ok Coral when actors became Rodeo King and Jesse of course with blanks.

But shooting ranges galore did spring up for gun enthusiasts, this was Texas, full of rattlers, Comanches and rustlers.

And a train station bult for golfers to be taken in pink

Cadillac's, well Chelsea had got the Franchise for taxing them to the beautiful golf mansion, bigger than Martha's folly.

The cafes opened on High Street, Chelsea hired latrine attendants and put the price of using a mobile latrine to five dollars.

What if you could not pay, see that cactus over yonder with the rattlers sleeping under it, go pee on it.

Chelsea was some businesswoman.

And who saved the lawmen from The Commander in Chiefs Law?

Listen, mouth organ music.

The president awoke seeing an ape riding a donkey playing a mouth organ.

He knew he was dead and promised, "I repent, just take me away from this demon on a donkey," and he meant every word.

Now ape was a Gigantopithecus and over nine feet tall, big by Texan standards.

"Do not do that apes giggle," but was too late as the ape ate all the golf balls and then carried Mr. President away on a shoulder, apes were going to the moon with OTHERS.

"GHFTY," apes saying, "I want my million or else."

So, who saved apes from the flame throwers, taxidermist D.I.Y. kit, a ticket to New York Zoo to join a dancing lion, be rescued by penguins and sent back to this tale of action and adventure.

And that spaceship landed on High Street and a door opened.

A bright blinding light shone out.

Figures appeared.

Little green men, who knows, the light was so blinding.

Mouth organ music was played well and a screaming girl, "Daddy Kins save me."

The Dire Wolfs ran by her shredding some of her shoes and skirt.

Then the shaper shifters ran by shredding the rest.

"DADDY KINS," loud then, "what nice blue eyes you have," and the mouth organ music stopped.

"That one of ours?" Mr. President.

"Yes Sir."

"We cannot shoot it down?"

"No sir and your daughter is aboard sir."

Silence, he knew, but the aliens did not, **hell had boarded their ship**.

And apes overheard it all as he still carried the president but when he tried to tell us what he eves dropped all he could say was, "Tidd juke luth?" That was Gigantopithecus for what he saw, can you understand him, we cannot.

"Take me to the golf club caddie," Mr. President thinking he could keep apes who did double as an electric caddy and secret service man in black bodyguard and take an assassins bullet meant for the president.

"Ouk," apes **understood that** and dropped the president and ran for the saucer where strange critters had boarded except for him.

"I want that caddie stuffed and mounted over the club house door," The President and explains why the ape was zigging and leaping to avoid the grenades, nets, tranquilizer darts and rubber arrows as the Comanche got into the act.

"Eek," the ape reaching the saucer door.

"Hugag," translated means, "let me in."

"Did he say please?"

"Ouk," the ape as a rubber lance bounced off his head.

Radioactive heat started escaping from engine exhausts as

the saucer readied to fly away to a happy place far away and the ape was not aboard.

And a mountain lion opened a porthole and reached out a paw for apes for animals have empathy for each other.

"TGHHJOYHU," the nine-foot ape that translated, "Saved, thanks pal, I owe you a double cheeseburger and fizzy drink."

And someone heaved the mountain lion from behind, so it fell upon apes and the porthole slammed shut, then opened and a vulture was stuffed out, then the port hole slammed shut.

Who threw them out?

And as the saucer was twenty feet above ground, apes tried remembering circus acts he seen on FLYERS blown onto the road, of an ape riding a lion by standing on the lions back.

Apes thought this a good idea as he could spring up and catch the windowsill.

Unfortunately, the mountain lion did not take kindly to a monster trying to break its back and went BERZERK.

"GHHK," the apes, "Christ what have I done, silly me," as the ape was shredded.

And the apes were going out happy as he remembered days gone by when he fought Sabre tooth tigers and lost.

And apes saw the outline of a ten-gallon hat against the porthole.

Had the wearer tossed the animal hanger ones out?

Remember he was a shrimp of a man and would have the day lights beaten out of him.

Also remember Nathan knew Kung Fu as good as Jackie.

And where was she?

"They were adoring me, those little green men, carrying dishes of Black Forest Cake on silver platters, fanning me with ostrich feathers grown in a laboratory aboard ship, spraying sweet smells onto my face so I passed out.

"It was the creaking porthole quickly that awoke me to trouble, I was surrounded by ten-gallon hats, I needed to think quick, I dug out of my elastics an oil can, waved it, then threw it yonder.

They followed; they were ashamed of the creaking porthole.

A bright girl does not need telling twice to RUN FOR YOUR LIFE."

"Wee," I went slipping away as the corridors were highly polished and in in front of me two lawmen blocking an open door.

"Do not blame me," I shouted into their backs as I crashed into them.

"We blame you," Nathan screamed.

"Yes, we blame the idiot that bumped into us," Clay screamed also.

"Why all this screaming, all I did was slide into their moons, think they did be grateful these lonesome boys," me Jackie but since I was holding onto them, I tried walking on solid floor that WAS NOT THERE. Just a drop to an opening below and Skin Walker ranch, how cute it looked all the tiny cows eating grass and Chupacabra sneaking up on them as vampires.

Now I screamed, "Jesus I repent, now save me," and I was a Buddhist.

Just in case you think my eyes sight that good, there was a lit-up billboard and flashing lights with 'Skin Walker ranch,' with an arrow pointing downwards.

The little green men thought of everything.

One drifted over to us as we fell and came right up to me.

It handed me a black Tulip, and because of the dark glassy big eyes saw no emotion there.

"A black Tulip, that is bad Jackie," Clay being full of knowledge.

"I thought we had a romance going," Jackie and looked at the lawmen with a smile that you would think she had taken out her false teeth.

The little green person had no clothes on, it had no sexual whatever and why Jackie gave that silly look to the lawmen.

"Is E.T. a boy or girl Jackie?" Nathan.

Jackie exploded, "I am heterosexual," and tried to Kung Fu Nathan.

A strange whistling sound and all understood the alien, it had said, "That is why we are dumping you; you are too HOT to handle, bye."

And the E.T. seemed to pull an indivisible plug and Jackie began to whoosh away, and in a situation like that you hold onto anything, so whooshed away with the lawmen's breaks.

E.T. shuddered shoulders as if laughing as was pointing at lawmen codpieces.

The boys covered their indignation.

"You are the law, arrest it," they heard Jackie as she was sucked out the exit door very fast heading to hit Skin Walker Ranch square during mid-day mealtime.

Is this SPLAT time for Jackie, has this rubbish turned violent to make up for the dribble, well, you do not have to read another thousand pages to find out.

E.T. were friendly and a light beam attached itself to her, so she was heard giggle as she landed in the swine pasture.

Her laughter turned to nasty swear words that brought the owners, para-normal investigators, television crew out from their mid-day meal of barbecued fries, and they said what you did say, "There is a shape shifter in the pig swill, get it on camera, we got to dissect it and stuff it, is it one of ours?"

"Ah so Jackie is here," and as she spun through the air shook herself like a dog, so the pig swill left her and went on them asking questions so they screamed.

"S**t pigswill on me, I will never get into Chelsea's tonight stinking of hog."

"The girls in the Purple Haze will do me up a hot bath," another who would be barred entry for he stank of boar swill, and pigs are clean animals and is us that keep them in confined spaces giving them barbecued Fries to eat causing colic and stinky runs to blame.

And by the time Jackie had chopped, poked, kicked, bit as allowed, the sixty people who had been sitting at the midday meal were groaning, moaning, wiggling worm like to be away and just plain unconscious, the midday meal was still hot waiting to be eaten.

After the meal Jackie was so distended parts she needed to sleep, and she had the choice of sixty beds and fell asleep in umber twelve.

Goodnight Jackie and we might visit you in the State Penal Colony chain gang where you might end up as these men and women you the daylights out on their mobiles phoned for help.

Notice they phoned proper law enforcement agencies, wake up Jackie and run.

CHAPTER 14 SAUCER LIFE.

Wonderbra Woman

There was a throne aboard the saucer reserved for important personages the E.T.'s might discover when they went across space.

SHE SAT UPON IT.

Yes her.

A queue of little green folk waited for her to pick from trays they carried, mirrors, lipsticks, fake eye lashes, mobile phones, and empty trays for those items SHE had finished with.

A hundred yards at the end of the queue a man no longer in a black suit but changed into a navy-blue one-piece tight stretchy suit, a badge with stars and planets was on his chest, a mouth organ hung about his neck.

An E.T. who looked important because it wore dark glasses stood beside him.

Alaskan Woman and Wonder Bra Woman stood as their guards, so did about a hundred little green E.T.'s.

And all forgot about the hapless lawmen because they were hapless.

"Blow it a kiss Nathan, this one likes you," Clay still suspended way above the exit Jackie went out.

"Bret," Nathan not good at blowing kisses.

E.T. just stared at him with those big glazed black eyes, then clicked a finger and drifted away taking the lawmen with it.

"Why am I going friend?" Clay worried not into party games.

"You are Otterman, do something?" Nathan.

Clay the darling had to think hard how he turned I not Otterman, that squeaky cute man-eating otter nine feet tall and was indoors so no one knew if the Otterman was house trained?

Let us find out?

Nathan remembered just in time as a door opened laced with pink curtains opened.

A familiar smell reached him but being Nathan did not recognize it.

A pity.

"I remember, kick me Nathan best friend, spit on me best friend, poke my eyes best friend, gas me best friend, make jokes that the last women Chelsea and Martha are your secret nighttime cooks so I can turn into Otterman best friend," Clay pleaded as he was remember a pacifist and needed help to lose it upstairs.

"If I do those things, we will not be best friends," Nathan passing through the pink lace curtains and the familiar scent overcame him, so he swooned.

"You have killed my best friend," Clay just as a familiar voice came to him.

"Hello Boy."

"Who could this be?"

"Squeak," came from Otterman, nine feet tall and had to squat to scratch fleas, then saw purple, Chelsea had boxes full of opened purple lingerie, XXX, postcards of home, Texan microwave instant meals, glass beads and herself to sell to E.T.

Delia had arrived in space.

"Mm, possibilities, but where is Clay," and Chelsea thought to the E.T. who had brought the boys to her.

The little green thingmabob hid behind her and pointed at the Otterman peeing against a wall plant.

"Clay darling," Chelsea had years of experience calming down Terlinguans with too much of her XXX in their bellies and too much of their dollars in her cash machines.

Anyway, the Otterman picked Nathan up between its teeth and looked at Chelsea, memory flashes of a time in the back of a 4x4 with Nathan giving him a middle finger and waving a purple bra at him flooded the peanut size brain of the otter advancing upon Chelsea.

The little whatever behind her had vanished, where had it gone, to the latrine as nerves had overcome the bowels?

To hide under the bed?

To get help?

"Smooch kiss," Chelsea with her lips and produced a carboard cut out of a leg.

The Otterman looked down at the thing in its mouth then back at the cut out.

"Thud," was the sound of Nathan hitting a wall as the Otterman humped the cutout.

"You are going to the zoo on Planet ABC my dear," and Chelsea unzipped herself and she was now a beautiful green E.T.

The product of hybrid breeding between E.T.'s and humans.

She was now Wonder Chelsea and a black cape hung from

her shoulders and to promote sales, she wore a purple bra.

And they came and took Otterman away who calmed down and became Clay as he was tossed into a cage with a sign on it.

"Otterman, King of the Otters," and a sponge dipped in wine in a greasy bucket for him to drink but would need to be a thirsty Otterman to squeeze moisture from that sponge, my it been lying there decades with creepy crawlies on it.

*

It was the giggling, slurping, bone crunching sounds that alerted Clay to the fact he might not be alone.

It was almost pitch dark.

Something kept poking his nose.

This time he caught it, his humane vegetarian beliefs stopped him pulling the wings of whatever had been poking his nose.

"Just as well, it was a light switch pull on off cord giggle and did like you to know the other giggling's were not made by me BUT THEM, those you can see now clay has LIGHT.

Clay was indeed in a zoo, a pet's petting area where cages of Chupacabra waited for him as a blood supper.

There must have been a hundred of them and he had only eight pints of blood.

"Tonka," Clay murmured.

Give him credit, he did not pee or do windy from the thought of approaching disaster.

He was Clay who was frozen with dread, so his bladder and innards were frozen.

"My pets, we have the means to turn you into one dearest Clay, but we will not, that please you," Chelsea her voice demanding so Clay defrosted.

"He ogled; the bum ogled. Giggle not amused giggle"

"But I do want to know what makes you tick Otterman, how does that sound Clay?" Chelsea and from nowhere pinged this note at him that bounced off his forehead.

Clay picked it up and took a long time bending down to pick up the note.

"The bum was ogling again."

"The key is mental, be at mine for cooking lessons later," and Chelsea blew a smooch and Clay involuntary jumped to catch it with pert lips.

"Where was the bucket, I want to puke giggle."

And behind Wonder Chelsea Clay saw a small man, he was fitting a new ten-gallon hat on his head, and turned to look at Clay, and their eyes met.

"Clay saw a 4x4 with Nathan in the passenger seat giving him a middle finger and waving a purple bra at him. Lay began to tremble, then shake violently so otter fleas flew off him onto concerned curious little green men who then ran amok scratching.

"Fleas was something new to them giggle."

And as Chelsea pinned a sheriff star onto Nathan's badge and pinched his cheeks so they glowed, then patted his head, and stuck a rubber dog chew between his lips, then picked him up effortlessly and carried him away to the control room to watch the world through the viewing glass as the little green men saw it, a world contaminated by polluting humans needing alien vets.

They had the means aboard ship.

Why Chelsea was a product of hybridization to evolve a better human race.

And Chelsea sat into a large swivel chair, remember she was a big girl with long insured legs, and patted Nathan on her lap.

And Nathan was content where he lay, what man would not

be?

Had he forgotten his best friend?

And Nathan was making purring sound and a little green alien held up a gold dish full of cream and he licked it all up.

"The bum knew when he was onto a good thing, Clay was absent, he had Chelsea the greenish E.T. all to himself. "I am puking Nathan on you giggle, better to puke on Fili Pek as being in Spirit it will have effect, Fili Pek come here so I can puke on you, giggle and he will come as adores me, and he has not come, must credit him with more intelligence than I do, and beat the ectoplasm out of him when I get him giggle."

"Your best friend Nathan?"

And "Area 51 is always grateful for the gifts you give AJAX Martian," and the speaker blew cigar rings and a mouth organ to played to communicate with the aliens.

The little green men had no mouths, just big black stare you out eyes that gave you the CREEPS.

And hundreds of little green aliens pushed a silent throne up to the viewing screen next to Chelsea and SHE sat in it pinging grape seeds at the aliens who carried spittoons for the grape seeds, seeds they would plant and grow into vineyards aboard ship, ready to send back to earth in a rewilding project.

And it was SHE who annoyed at the attention Chelsea was getting from a purring Nathan aimed, then pinged a grape seed all the way into a big black eye of an E.T. standing next to a wheel.

Of course, it hurt, SHE could not miss, those E.T. eyes were so big.

Anyway, the wheel was for show, he steered the ship with **thought waves** and now the thought waves was PAIN, not left or right, up, or down, but PAIN, and the E.T. groped and pulled a lever that had some skull and cross bones drawn over it.

It could only mean trouble.

And trouble came.

The lever had opened the cages in the petting zoo.

Guess who was FREE?

A gush of water with wobbly jelly fish slid across the floor, stinging bare ankles as the E.T. wore no clothes and showed no genitals so there.

Not only stinging jelly fish but octopus who being curious animals with eight legs ending in suckers had to wrap about the bellies of E.T.'s and shook them this way and that to see if they rattled or squeaked, and examine their sexes, these are OCTOPUS*, really, could fool me?

Alien octopus so EARTH GIRLS BEWARE.

Earth boys BEAWRE also.

Equal opportunities in this tale.

And a water droplet splashed upon the forehead of Nathan, a gentle soul, a lawman of the old west, a man who never went to a religious house, he had better stuff to cook and cook was the word, cooking Lacunae and opening a stubborn jar of green olives with his teeth and able to as has gold filings, and wobbles the mattress so the cheese is split and the camping stuff sets alight Martha's bed, then her castle and Nathan better run.

He at last had found true happiness with an alien.

Chelsea who now and again turned her head to flicker out a foot long purple forked tongue, but Nathan was happy, he never noticed, nor the vampire fangs Chelsea was having trouble keeping in her mouth.

Who would save Nathan dreaming of marriage and babies, a garden to weed, a lawn to mow, the dog litter to scope up, who would save Nathan from having little green kids and being tickled by s snake tongue and being rushed to emergency after

Chelsea had sucked 7 pints of his blood; Chelsea was being realistic, sucking 8 would kill Nathan, why she was not a murderers, just a good businesswoman.

And the water droplet alerted Nathan to HELL.

"My what big biceps you have Otterman, here change places with Nathan," and Chelsea used leg movements to flip Nathan up into the air where he span, so was dizzy and unfocused.

"Otterman," he mumbled as memories of giving Clay a middle finger in a 4x4 and waving a purple bra at him, so "my darling Clay was not hallucinating, forgive me Clay giggle."

And Otterman remembered and was to catch a falling Nathan and tear, shred, bite, and rip apart his best friend over this green alien girl, *"well girls are always girls and just ask any sailor that giggle."*

And Chelsea looked down as something warm, wet, and smelt off a wet dog lay in her lap.

A Dire wolf wanted some of the attention Nathan got, so Chelsea exploded and threw the wolf off her, so it spans in the air next to Nathan.

"Who is responsible for this?" Chelsea roared and the little green men cleared a path of vision and pointed at a human person.

And Clay leaped into the air, some thirty feet as being Otterman was capable off that feat and with both hands and arms snatched two bodies out of the air.

"Was Clay a sort sighted Otterman, could he not tell the difference between a Dire-Wolf and his ex-best friend, *"obviously not giggle."*

And laughing hysterically ran into the ship's corridors to rip, shred, bite, and tear apart two breathing bodies he held.

And while he escaped the little green men not looking at whom they pointed to, pointed at the source of exciting mouth organ music as exciting tales need musical atmosphere.

Johnny Christy stopped playing and negatively shook his head.

The alien AJAX beside him side stepped so there was a safe distance between himself and Johnny.

The little green aliens now looked at whom they had pointed as the source of trouble and mentally said, "WHOOPS."

And Chelsea strode along to Johnny making sure her insured legs were on display.

Johnny and all the aliens were transfixed on those limbs.

And Wonder Bra Woman and Alaskan Woman glared at Johnny not Chelsea for he was ogling.

"Hell has no fury like a woman scorned giggle, just what attention did he give these promoted bedroom cooks? He soothed them with mouth organ music and excited them with fast banjo strumming.

Not enough Johnny, a woman needs imported Belgian chocolates with the custom duty still attached, French knickers, Italian serenaded, laboratory grown mink furs and your credit cards, and you give them music, giggle, he is going to die young.

Click, click, wake up Johnny giggle, got to forgive him, never seen legs like hers, nor have I, carboard cut outs, yes carboard cuts outs, do you think Chelsea did risk injury to her own shaven smooth legs, no, for starters the insurance did go up."

And Chelsea tickled his chin as memories of cooking, washing his soiled undies, soaking his sweaty socks, ironing his starchy black shirts, stitching the rips in his cod piece, having to travel miles to a musical shop to buy banjo strings, and new read along nighttime stories to keep the bogyman away for JOHNNY.

And Wonder Bra Woman and Alaskan Woman read her thoughts as woman can read the twitch of a lip, the flash of red in an eye, the herpes scabs flaking, and agree with each other about Johnny secret agent 001.

"Memories can be good or bad giggle; you decide and then tell Johnny what to do next?

And she was about to smooch his neck where she did expose those vampire teeth.

"Was she the mother of the Chupacabra, were these devil dogs brought to earth by E.T. What profit could an alien businesswoman obtain from these vampire dogs roaming Texas, well, they BROUGHT IN THE PARANORMAL HUNTERS, SELFIES, HOEPFUL TAXIDERMISTS, TELEVISION CREWS, A President who was to build a children's petting zoo for them in Terlingua, and these folks and a million other tourists did buy spend dollars in her establishment with the pink curtains and did her XXX.

And below mercury was mined and shipped back to the mother ship, the saucer they were all in to be taken back to PLANET AJAX in a far Away Galaxy.

Chelsea was some smart businesswoman.

And she on a throne was not happy she was no longer the center of attention flicked a grape seed at the boson at the wheel with a bandage over one eye, now he did need to band aids.

The President's daughter was an excellent aimer.

So never missed.

"Oh dear, the bosun holding his eyes sent the wrong thoughts to the wheel and the saucer nose dived at six thousand miles an hour.

That is some speed and explains all these U.F.O. multiple sightings, where the saucers zoom and stop just like that.

Well, SHE was no longer in her throne as THRUST had sent her tumbling into the air, but SHE was a trained cheer leader and with a twirl, so her white ankle socks showed, and white other stuff, band aids as those hairy animals aboard ship needed defleaed, and since the Dire-Wolfs were prehistoric so were the fleas, big chitinous fleas.

Not to mention the prehistoric ticks.

"And the ape and others left behind should be happy they were not on the ship giggle, especially the ape as Gigantopithecus are hairy, just ask anyone who has seen a Big Foot.

"Big, hairy and stinky," the answer.

And suddenly on the viewing screen sharks, cod, whales and the ship were still diving under the waves to 'Davy Jones's Locker.'

"Well hello baby," yes, he said it and probably one of his opening lines to all his dish washers, and Johnny saw $1,000,000 reward from the President who never expected to pay out, why he did get her back free or better NEVER accept.

"Hello baby they s**t me all over," an annoyed Chelsea and should never have said and thought that when the room was full of Dire-Wolves and Chupacabra and shape shifters, yes, they were in on the act.

This saucer was a regular visitor to 'Skin Walker ranch.'

"So, Johnny was saved by what doggy animals leave behind all over Chelsea, well she did ask for it giggle."

The marvelous thing was that the aliens had perfected anti-gravity, those invisible lines that when you drop Nathan off a roof he floats down as is on an anti-gravity line, and if you open a window and push him sideways, he will enter a gravity line and speed down and need emergency real soon.

*"Anti-gravity, why men could walk amongst the clouds if they **illuminated these lines** like cat eyes on the side of a road, giggle."*

And Nathan was speaking gibberish, "Clay please do not eat me, honest nothing ever happened in the passenger seat of the 4x4. I found the purple bra in the glove compartment and a card, oh Clay stop dribbling saliva over me and listen, the card was Johnny's calling card with his secret contact numbers and a message, 'EAT ME AFTER REMEMBERING CONTACT NUMBERS.'

Clay are you listening to me, of course not, you are thinking of shredding your best friend and burying his bones as a snack later, bad Otterman," Nathan out of words.

"Gr," the Dire-Wolf with better judgement and snapped its big jaws on Clay's whatever so that froze clay dead.

Then Chelsea running screaming asking for a shower, a bath, a horse trough, little green volunteers to scrape the animal droppings of her ran into Clay.

And the stink of her added to the Dire-Wolf bite brought Clay back to his human shape.

He dropped Nathan as Clay's mouth was made for chewing hot dogs dripping American yellow mustard and licking ice cream, not holding Nathan.

And Clay made a funny face as a silver filling popped out with Nathan.

"Another grudge, what gives with friendship these days giggle?"

And Clay looked down at his codpiece in a Dire-Wolf's mouth.

Chelsea stopped screaming, what was going on was more interesting than seeking her servants to bath her, of course female servants but then these aliens with no obvious genitals could be either mentally.

"As Jesus said, there are no sexes in heaven, just spirits like me and Fili Pek and reminds me, where is he, Jesus Christ I was so engrossed like Chelsea never noticed the 'jerk' wrapped about my right leg, get off me giggle."

And the Dire-Wolf being an angel shifted its jaws while looking up at Clay.

Clay made funny sounds.

Now, was the saucer hitting the seabed that broke up the party here.

Clay flew over Chelsea with his pet Dire-Wolf.

Nathan held up a hand to volunteer to wash Chelsea.

Then guilt and memories of past adventures filled Nathan, yes, he was an imbecile who crawled under Chelsea's feet and noticed she had webbed feet for the first time.

His children he realized did have webbed toes, he peeked at her fingers, he was in awe, they were webbed to, why had he never noticed, and then the cardboard cut legs attached to the webbed toes stood on him and he looked straight up and saw the answer to why he never noticed her fingers and toes, he was ogling insured appendages and so forgot all about webbing, or did he, was he leaving that surprise to his BST FRIEND CLAY, as in love all is fair as in war.

Where was he crawling to?

To save his best friend.

"And an angelic choir sang about him, orbs of light floated past his eyes blinding him, making him useless as a savior.

And the side wall opened so the Dire-Wolf in fear of drowning, let go of Clay places and climbed to the top of Clay's head.

"Something tells us either tis Dire-Wolf could not swim or was afraid of getting wet giggle."

Trumpets blared, drums beat, the boots of soldiers marching, an army was coming.

Clay changed places with the Dire-Wolf.

Chelsea used Nathan as a towel to wipe herself somewhat clean.

From elastic she produced the most expensive laboratory made perfume. Aliens did not use animals to test drugs and perfumes, they had brilliant minds that build saucers so could easily stick atoms and molecules here and there in a test tube to get a perfume The President's daughter, SHE above did crave for.

And from her cleavage a mouth spray, mint essence, grown in the fields the aliens cultivated.

Where?

Keep reading to find out.

But the saucer did not flood with sea water and sharks, these aliens knew their engineering and a tube had extended from an underwater city to the saucer.

And these men were coming to find out why the saucer had landed so fast and badly.

They were about to meet HER, better called SHE

"Who are you, come to give me presents?" She is being carried by the green aliens.

Behind her Johnny and AJAX Boss alien, and behind them Wonder Bra Woman and Alaskan Woman carrying a polished shield that Johnny and AJAX stood upon, they were leaders, chieftains, and the two women giving all an example in subjection, serfdom, slavery, females belong in the cooking house, washroom, stuffing the vegan turkey at 'Thanksgiving,' yes two women who read each other's wrinkle movements for women can.

And the aliens carrying the throne with HER on it dumped it amongst the advancing aliens out of the connecting tube.

CONNECTING TO WHERE?

Do not be so nosy.

"Get your hand off my trainers creep," SHE screamed at the aliens.

"My Daddy Kins is the President of The American Golfers Association, you will now meet the men in Black," and SHE used her mobile hidden under her gold wristwatch.

The aliens stopped tying her trainer laces together and looked at one another.

They thought and laughed, "Men in Black," and suddenly they were here, Men in Black.

But they were green aliens in black overcoats and dark

glasses.

They all pointed at a sign on a wall.

"THIS SAUCER WAS MADE WITH THE CO-OPERASTION OF THE UNITED STATES OF AMERICA."

Nathan saluted.

Clay saluted.

The chupacabra entered, hundreds of them, these cages, well the beasts had nothing to do but, have you guessed.

"Gnaw bones, suck blood drinks, scratch fleas, lick bums, and be bored and so their doggy minds turned to milk shakes and ice cream cones would you believe? Giggle."

"Daddy Kins, you get your a**e here now or just wait till I get home," SHE as the Chupacabra by sheer weight of numbers pushed her and everyone else down the tube into a vast Emerald City, hot air balloons floated in the sky with alien television crews filming, a stuffed lion waved greetings, a tin man ran for it knowing better, and a straw man was floored and shredded some as the Chupacabra used his straw innards as a latrine.

And a pair of red shoes danced by themselves just before kicking every one of those devil dogs' places, so they yelped back to the safety of bright green woods, with delicious apples growing on them, and an old woman poisoning some as she mumbled, "Why is everyone more beautiful than me?"

"Time to get back to Terlingua boys," The two wonder women gesticulating for our boys to follow.

And without question they did, why because wonder women do not dress decently, and the boys were ogling.

So never entered this underwater city of aliens.

And followed the wonder women like sheep to an 'EMERGENCY EXIT,' AND BELOW IT A SIGN, 'THE SUMBERSIVILE WAS MADE IN BOSTON WITH THE

CO-OPERATION OF ALIENS, TRUSTED FRIENDS OF THE

UNITED STATES OF AMERICA.'

Two robotic marines came out of the wall marching to music, gave Big Bang Time, then went back into the walls.

"Wow," Nathan gob sucked.

"Tonka awesome," Nathan unbelieving.

And the two girls fast as a spinning atom changed out of the tight ripping wonder comic clothes and now were female men in black.

"We were recruited by Johnny," Wonder Bra Woman burning her bra, so the sprinklers came on.

"Only for a day as he wanted to show us girls were not the equal of men, for a day, Johnny just wait to you turn up for din dins," Alaska Woman.

Nathan rubbed his eyes and peered hoping he did not miss anything, but the girls had been faster than an electric toy train changing their clothes.

Clay held out his hands to catch the falling bra ashes, "I am free of purple bras, thank you Tonka."

The girls looked at him as if he was an imbecile and would make sure when he visited for cooking lessons silver bullets, tranquilizer darts, a handy back door also to throw Clay out when he mumbled things like, "Tonka has saved me from the curse of 'The Purple Bra,' then squeak loudly as he fought not to change into Otterman.

And the girls in black entered the submersible and shut the door.

"Knock, knock."

"Whose there?"

"Us so please let us in," Nathan and Clay.

"Cannot do," the reply from a speaker, "because of them."

"Them?" Our curious boys.

And the submersible pinged away into the depths to head to the surface without the boys.

And curiosity made the lawmen turn and look.

The whole population of the underground city was heading their way.

Upfront monkeys in uniform and witches on levitating brooms.

"She yours?" a witch asked as the aliens lacked mouths.

"Tonka thank you," Clay seeing a Cadillac as a patrol car with stereo playing 'El Condor.'

"I can have my own R.V. and an automatic meal vendor, who needs those girls anyway," Nathan.

And strange looking small people dressed in Germanic leathers dumped a gagged, taped SHE at their feet.

The boys banged their heads together reaching for the million dollars.

The sound of a mouth organ was heard, and the submersible reversed back into the loading bay.

"And the girls in black relieved our boys of a million dollars. In other words, it was so easy to roll the gagged taped President's daughter aboard the submersible, putting a knee in here, knuckles here, a middle finger there, a spray of perfume ingo the yes, a clothes peg on a tongue, for the girls in black knew how to treat a woman who just never shut up.

"Now if it had been men rolling her aboard, they did have carried the President's daughter, pawing here, pawing there, ogling here, ogling there, even quickly ripping the masking tape off that mouth, the chains off the wrists and ankles, to wipe the grime off her shirt, to let the spoil monster free because that is what men do with a captive woman.

"Ouch," Johnny rushing into a closed submersible door as the girls in black knew a million split two ways did not go very far, so

Johnny could beg. They were girls who had awoken to their value as women who could vote sensibly.

Our boys began to cry, penniless again.

"You are fried, hear me, fired," Johnny at the departing submersible.

And the small people made a clearing and a man with a white beard appeared standing on a floating disc.

"Want home to Kansas do we lads?" he asked the crying men.

"I want where that submersible is going," Johnny and played his mouth organ.

"Did I ask you," the old man on the disc, it was just not Johnny's day.

"Come with me," the msn on the disc said and the small people helped Clay and Nathan to follow by pushing, pinching, kicking, probing, and pawing them along.

Johnny walked tall and proud, no one probed, pinched, and pawed him, he was still 001.

And the boys filled with awe when they walked a yellow brick road into the Emerald City.

Aliens waved at them from balconies, threw flowers at them, took selfies with them, and the procession came to a stop in a square, made of marble so would have been cold if not for the heating underneath it.

The aliens liked their warmth.

"I will send you back where you want to go, just take these with you," and the old man indicated a lion with a shy face, a tin man needing oiled and a straw man needing straw, and he stank of Chupacabra pee.

The boys looked at each other and slapped each other to wake up.

"In that balloon you will travel home, hello where is that balloon," and he looked up and heard mouth organ music drifting away with the balloon through an exit and into the sea, of course the basket was waterproof and the size of an ice hockey stadium, see the aliens had taught the Texans everything should be big.

"Looks like you are staying with us till the end of time," the old man.

The boys slumped.

"Only joking, I can sell you another submersible that will take you till the end of time to pay off," the old man and pointed with a palm and BEHOLD, it was mini saucer with a pilot.

And the pilot turned and smiled at them, pointing her lips in smooches.

It was the human Chelsea.

"She will take you back to Terlingua, and we are not worried if you talk about what you have seen, no one will believe you and if you keep insisting on talking, you will be locked up in a funny farm," the old man.

And the boys knew he was right.

No one believed them when they said they saw Big Foot and so never got the reward for discovering Big Foot.

They were labelled 'Cryptic Hunters,' and that explained all.

CHAPTER 16 OTTERMAN

Otterman shreds his regulation Deputy Sheriff Attire and plays with an alien with a beach ball and shredded clothes must be paid for out of wages, never mind, always a girl to cook, wash his diapers and mend his shreds as girls just adore otters.

Now since Nathan was the sheriff he got to ride upfront with the pilot and Clay being a deputy got to sit in the rear seats.

Separated from those upfront by a force field.

And Clay remembered a 4x4 and was Nathan turning round and giving him a middle finger.

Was that a purple bra thrown at the force field, so the bra sizzled, frizzled, and vaporized?

And Clay shook all over, so his cod piece wobbled, and Chelsea saw all in her rear-view mirror as a good pilot checks her mirrors not just to put on a fresh smear of red lipstick, and Chelsea put the lipstick away and sprayed her mouth with mint freshness.

Nathan walked up to the force field and showed Clay his open hands.

Too late, Otterman was back and Chelsea being an imp had

turned off the force field.

"Oh dear, my advice to Nathan was run giggle."

And Otterman lept at his hated memory and sailed over Nathan because sometimes it pays to be small, and Otterman never saw where he landed as he was staring at Nathan.

But landed on softness that knew how to deal with an Otterman.

Why Chelsea played with Chupacabra, Dire-Wolfs and other critters for she was an alien who had been to 'Skin Walker Ranch' many times, in flying saucers, perhaps the one you filmed for a paranormal show.

She was Chelsea, a real wonder woman, who needed a phone booth, mobile latrine, the back of your pickup, or down an open manhole to change from human to alien and back again.

And Otterman liked the taste of red lipstick and Chelsea let him lick the tube, just to get on the good side of Otterman.

And Nathan noticed something very important.

Who was driving?

And the saucer just like that was over Terlingua and F-16's zoomed it.

Nathan waved at the human pilots who gave him a middle finger back.

"Can we shoot it down Commander in Chief?" The human air force pilots asked and just as well Nathan never heard.

And a golf ball bounced off the saucer.

"Who is flying that saucer, I want him sent back to Mexico," Mr. President throwing his club at the saucer, but the saucer was too high, so the club came back, for what goes up comes down.

"Do we get a medic sir," a caddie somersaulting in the air and the governor replied, "No," and sent his own caddie somersaulting in the air to put his golf ball down the hole, and if that was the President's ball yonder, to drop it in the sand pit.

"All is fair in a golf game giggle."

And a saucer landed on a ranch.

The occupiers of the ranch house came out with television crews.

This is what they had been waiting for to start their new paranormal season with.

And filmed Chelsea's legs as she descended from the saucer to the grass.

Of course, if she had used a ladder her legs did have been covered.

She was a businesswoman and was about to charge these humans royalty fees.

And no one noticed two pale faces peek out the saucer door.

Nathan and Clay.

And they puked as were air sick.

Someone from the television crew threw them a mop and bucket.

"Ouch," as the mop hit home.

"Cur that hurt," as the heavy bucket stroke a small man.

*

"These boots were not made for walking," Clay complained.

"Friend, see that smudge on the horizon, that is Terlingua were we will be made welcome, heroes for getting the rustlers," Nathan and gritted his teeth as a true cowboy would, and pulled up his rousers now dry and hot under the merciless BIG Texan sun.

Clay was not so sure, he had a memory of walking this way before, then a golf ball hit Nathan square in the middle of his forehead.

He did not even get a chance to say, "I been hit by something hard, goodbye friend Clay."

Nope, he went down like a sack of potatoes.

The white golf ball bounced onto Clay's nose making him cross eyes looking at it.

Just like loud music and cheer leaders twirling in the air.

Cheeky cheerleaders flashing their ankle socks and pinging Clay's ears, pulling his trousers way back so his regulation navy blue deputy underwear showed and then the trousers ripped as had been through hell and needed a seamstress.

Well, they were out in the Pan Handle so there was not any seamstress here, just dung beetles waiting for them to pooh, vultures for them to die, folk to scavenge their clothes off them, boots, and socks also, leaving them starker's'.

"DRINK COLD FIZZY AT MO'S," banners waved in front of Clay.

"AMERICAN HOT DOGS AT JOE'S."

"BANK WITH TERLINGUA."

Then they were gone, the golf ball also.

Clay was left with outstretched hands imploring food and drink.

"Sorry we do not take credit, cash only," a sweet girly voice drifted to him.

Clay went 'TONKA is a girl?'

About a hundred yards from where he started, he stopped panting hard, dripping sweat from everywhere so soon would stink bad.

"Hello handsome, want a lift?" Martha asked.

"We got no spare horses, you can hold the tail and hope for the best it done its business," Mr. Kit in a well pressed gunslinger outfit, he had been promoted to Martha's never mind, yes to tell Martha fairy tales now Granny Smith was gone.

And Clay held the horses tail and they were off.

Mr. Kit drank noisily spilling lots as he never forgot Martha had once the 'trots' for Clay and still might have.

He was a male slug descended from Adam's line.

"Clay dear, you not forgetting someone?" Martha so songbirds came with her words making Mr. Kit murderous.

"Tonka my best friend Nathan," Clay no half a mile from Nathan.

And Nathan was easy to spot as was covered in vultures, dung beetles and scavenger folk.

Clay started running back but his 'TONKA' tantrum had drained him, he needed a caffeine drink.

Instead, Mr. Kit rode up to him, here this will give you energy," and dropped a baby rattler onto Clay's covered moons.

Clay ran fast after that.

"Why you are jealous Kit, how sweet," Martha and leaned over and smooched.

The rattler was made of rubber and had sticky appendages so was stuck to Clay's moons and explains why he was running, and as fast as he ran, he could not get away from the rattler.

The vultures flew up as he neared and collapsed UPON Nathan.

The vultures, dung beetles and scavenging folk returned.

"See what a good friend Clay was, he was protecting Nathan with his own body giggle."

Who did save the lawmen from a stripping out on the Pan Handle?

A dark shadow covered them.

A condor of the famous song.

The saucer come back.

No was a hot air balloon some secret agent had stolen from an old man in an undersea Emerald City were aliens thrived.

See, secret agents can do what they want and get away with it as all is a secret and not admissible in the courts.

Cold fizzy drink was dribbled down from the hot air basket and revived the lawmen.

"Give us a lift Johnny," Clay asked.

"Yes, Johnny our feet are blistered, we are itching dung beetles, the vultures have c*****d over us, and we need a bath Johnny," Nathan.

And would you allow stinky men into your clean parlor?

Of course, not so explains why the hot air balloon headed towards Terlingua.

But help was still at hand as an alien craft appeared blowing hot radioactive air onto the tired lawmen.

And a stairway appeared and there stood Cindy Lou and Wendy Lou.

There boys were halfway up that ladder when the girls vamoosed back into the alien craft and darted towards Terlingua.

Would you allow smelly men into your clean parlor?

But heaven was merciful as Clay held onto the rim of the stairway and Nathan onto his breaks.

The vultures followed them not giving up on a meal yet.

Below a pack of Chupacabra giggled after them.

The dung beetles were hard put to keep up.

"Who will save my boys giggle, Fili Pek?"

And her name was Dolly, a mangy canine with a blood sucking habit that was heading for the bung from the new Terlingua 'Children's Petting Zoo.' Why, because she was a mangy canine with a blood sucking habit.

And she was in love with an ape that was riding a new tricycle as part of the monkey tea party in the 'Children's Zoo.'

And the ape was cycling hard as knew a mangy canine with a blood sucking habit was wanting to smooch with it.

And a 4x4 was coming this way also, and behind the wheel not a green-eyed girl but a green alien girl.

And the flying craft doors opened and jammed in Clay's fingers. Now when that happens our first instinct is not to say, "Whose there?" Or look out the porthole to see if a Johnny disguised as a bird was knocking or get ready the fold up mini paragliders to escape from Johnny, or heave heavy parachute rucksacks to the door if needed to throw out so the weight did rush Johnny to the ground without any time for him to put one on, and knowing Johnny did activate a hundred balloons sewn into his underwear so did land softly, he was Johnny Christy, no, your first instinct is to heave the door open scraping the skin of Clay's knuckles so her screamed and fell backwards.

"Oh, hello Nathan," he said seeing who held onto his breeks and added "Nathan saves me," but let us ask *"how giggle?"*

And heaven had pity upon the lawmen as SHE was thrown out of an unidentified flying craft.

"SHE just will not stop talking," Madam Wendy Lou formally Alaskan Wonder Woman holding her ears.

"Do this, I want this, clean my ears, yes enough," Cindy Lou formally Wonder Bra Woman.

"And was an easy thing to do, just open the craft 'EXIT' door and push her out, oaky, violently throw the B***H out," both girls and now we can ask the question, who is piloting this alien craft since you are busy with your hands?

"Not them giggle."

"Do something or Daddy Kins will have your lawmen badges off you," yes, SHE ordered our boys gliding to them as her cheerleader pleats acted as free fall parachutes partly opened.

Clay replied, "Madam, you are hanging onto my breeks, please let go."

"Of course, SHE did not, SHE was waiting for pornographic exposure.

"Madam, you are standing on my head, wiping your feet and leaving whatever those aliens were breeding in my hair," Nathan a worried man.

"What hair badly," SHE replied to Nathan and "stop pulling your breeks up BOY," SHE ordered a decent man.

And a vulture remembered Clay who fed it Nathan's cooking so was not kindly disposed to Clay so ignored him.

And remembered Nathan who fed it Clay's cooking so was not kindly disposed to him.

So took SHE, and all Terlingua came out and looked heavenwards towards the profanity source.

"It is your daughter Mr. President, we better send in an F-16 to get her back," a GIRL IN BLACK.

Mr. President was tempted, they could say an accidental missile strike against a St. Helena weather Balloon, but then he remembered her mother who had taught the brat her ways and shivered.

The mother needed to take a cruise ship that would meet an accidental torpedo and he did be free of them both.

No more, "Give me your credit cards, I have a headache, go sleep with one of your girlfriends," a reminder to him they knew divorce lawyers, and "if you want us to pose smiling in election photos, the title deeds to Great Britain."

No, send those two lawmen after her, that is what they get paid for," Mr. President and had he forgotten a million-dollar reward to have her back.

"*Yes, he had he silly Billy.*"

And the prehistoric ape man on a tricycle balanced on the handlebars and caught Nathan legs and pulled him hard down.

The sound of denim brass buttons pinging away, and

regulations deputy trousers dropped over Nathan.

"Help me best friend a hairy thingmabob has me," Nathan sliding down between the ape man's legs so shouted, "CLAY."

But Clay was balancing on thin air as the wind blew his opened regulation trousers up and away, he went to land on the back of 4x4.

Chelsea in her human make up smiled at him.

"Told you heaven was smiling on Clay giggle, but what about Nathan, yes, the small man?

And a battered Fili Pek as a white orb floated in front of the ape man's eyes who blinded and frightened, in other words 's******g' himself, aggressively steered left, then right, no left, no right, upwards, yes as threw the tricycle away and with-it Nathan.

"Ouch," Clay in the back of the 4x4 as a tricycle landed on him.

And Nathan turned to face him from the passenger seat and gave him a middle finger and waved a purple bra at him.

"How did Nathan fly thought the open passenger seat window, the wind carried him, and the purple bra, Chelsea had recently changed from a green webbed alien into a human and was now obviously braless.

Never mind Dolly leaped and landed on Clay licking him as was glad to see him but not Otterman whom Clay was changing into.

Just as well he did as a vulture fed up with HER was hearing, "put me down or else roast bird for dinner tonight," so the bird did.

"Put her down giggle.

And Fili Pek went to save her, how, he was a spirit orb, he was ogling the ankle socks and when he got back to me, readers look the other way for heaven knows how to deal with his sorts, they give them to me giggle."

And SHE was caught by an angry Otterman sixty yards up for the Otterman.

could leap and SHE marveled, she had been bettered as a cheerleader and knew with a veterinary haircut, shave, trim and false boobs and tights whoever this creature was, could work for Daddy Kins as a caddie on the golf course, and leap and catch Daddy Kin's bad shots as the balls headed for the long grass and snakes and homeless sleepers.

So, Clay had sixty yards to fall and ogle what he held and being Otterman could not understand a command, order, demand SHE was giving, until he landed in the back of the 4x4.

And the wind carried them in case you were wondering how sixty yards up they came down into the back of a fast-moving 4x4.

Which stopped so Clay flew against the glass partition of the vehicle.

Nathan turned and saw moons, decently covered in elastics as this is a clean tale and Clay's head was not where your unclean minds think it was, it was down at HER ankle socks, see, no afterlight suggestions in this tale.

"It is them bums, just takes one.

"Yes, them that burned our city down," another.

"Will Chelsea open her establishment and give us XXX?" Another.

"Yes, I am thirsty and XXX always makes a lynching easier to swallow," another.

And in response a vehicle door opened and insured legs popped out, cardboard cut outs, insured of course and there she was, the businesswoman.

"Nothing in life is free, 5% discount on the fifth drink so hurry up before the offer ends," Chelsea pulling up her stockings from the suspenders.

Of course, that did the trick, and the street was emptied as folks cramped into hers and those that failed to enter, well Purple Haze sold her XXX.

They were lynching lawmen tonight.

"Daddy kins," a daughter happy to see her father.

"Sweetie pie," a lying father who would have liked to say, "Hell is back," but knew better. He knew all about wisdom as had been brought up on tales of smart rabbits and foxes.

"Mr. President, do we get the reward then?" Nathan being small and a protected species asked.

Mr. President looked down.

Girls in black circled the lawmen, and the lawmen did not object as they were ogling.

A smile crossed the president's face.

Out came a cheque book and a scribbler later he handed Nathan it.

$1,000,000 was in ink.

Clay opened mouth salivated upon it.

Nathan swatted Clay away.

A tricycle bell was not heard.

A hairy Hand with fingernails needing cleaned grabbed the cheque and the tricycle sped away.

"There are horses out back of the jailhouse," an overweight sheriff now in a new job as tour guide.

A bell sounded and a loudspeaker came on with flood lights, and there at one end of High Street, Jesse labeled as 'King of the Badmen," and at the other end of High Street, "Rodeo King," and "Who would be the King to walk away from the gun fight at the Terlingua Coral, tickets $20 each, children $10."

And the lawmen exited the handy back door of the jailhouse

and there were their original animals and a man on a golden horse playing a mouth organ.

"Spilt three ways lads, better hurry as that ape man is peddling fast back to Alaska," Johnny.

*

And a pack of Dire-Wolves not understanding why the ape man was making a dust trail investigated.

Well, the ape was taking a short cut across 'Skin Walker Ranch' as unable to read, could not read the signs, remember them, warning folk to stay away, signs that pointed the wrong way anyway.

So was asking for trouble and 'Shape Shifters' joined the giant wolves thinking a herd of bison was making the dust trail and food was available for their taunt stomachs.

And the rest of the Chupacabra not wanting to miss out on the action came to.

And the television crews, paranormal teams, tourists, hairy bikers, and alien hunters in their hundreds poured out of the ranch house and onto trek machines, horses, scooters, and electric bicycles and gave chase.

And behind them a horde of cheer leaders visiting from Terlingua's new golf courses.

They are being cheer leaders had merely visited to cheer the lonely folk up in the ranch house, as gets bored waiting for aliens and monsters you know.

And a mountain lion cheered seeing Clay back and ran after him.

And ahead trouble descended upon apes and "Boys I cannot see a thing, but my, I mean our money is in there somewhere, go get it," Johnny being smart did not want to spend his share of the million rewards on hospital bills as America does not have a National Health.

And out of the dust cloud ran Dolly and in her wet gums a cheque.

And Johnny did not wait for the imbeciles Nathan and Clay to return out of the dust cloud as he went after that cheque, by himself.

And yes, corned Dolly far away where Dolly knew no one did find her, except him, the best secret agent ever, 001.

"Doggy biscuit in it for the paper in your mouth dog," Johnny knowing nothing about Chupacabra.

And the vampire dog chewed the cheque as liked the taste of ink.

And Johnny forgot he was not wrestling a dog, but a vampire dog bred by aliens and the United States Government, why, ask them not me.

And Johnny stood there gleaming infected Chupacabra saliva, bleeding from puncture bites, and exposing himself rudely as the devil had ripped his tight clothing to shreds, so we can now ask, was Johnny wearing invisible clothing.

"And the cheque was signed, 'MICKY MOUSE.'

Silence.

Then Johnny knew he had been battered by a man deserving to be president for only such a person, man or female could be president of this great land full Chupacabra, Dire-Wolves, Big Foot, Comanche, and golf courses.

And HIM.

He was smiling also as her did get paid a million in expenses for this mission.

*

"Well, le left us the horses," Nathan looking east towards Virginia and in his hand a newspaper cutting, 'MOTHMAN STRIKES AGAIN.'

"I hear there are Big Foot there also, were-wolves and civil war ghosts, we cannot fail this time with so much paranormal activity," Clay rubbing an empty tummy.

And they headed that way followed by curious Chupacabra, Dire-Wolves, shape shifters and an ape, and Virginia would never forgive them.

A front page of the Terlingua reporter blew across the prairie in front of them.

A picture showed the famous quick draw lawmen who fought the rustlers at the Terlingua Coral, and cleaned up Terlingua, making it safe for tourists, canoeists, golfers, hot head chili eaters, music lovers, the other type of lovers, of Chelsea's XXX and Terlingua to show their gratitude paid for their horse drawn hurst and burial in the 'Pioneer Cemetery,' where you can buy flowers and lay them at their gravestones, the lawmen Sheriff Nathan Bottom Moons, and his Deputy Tonto Clay Eagle.

Terlingua welcomes tourists.

And a gopher took the paper down into a borrow to shred and make a cozy bed for Texan nights are cold.

Behind them, fed up with the new sounds of Terlingua, a mountain lion was seeking adventure so Clay would not be cold as Texan nights could be cold.

"What about Nathan, who would keep him warm, well who was he, oh you mean the small man, Fili Pek you got a job of hot air blower nights, come here you little sneak, giggle."

It was said an Irish leprechaun was seen at night while the lawmen slept filling their boots with gold, almost every night for six months so the boys were weighed down, the horses rebellious from carrying such weight, so our boys passing an abandoned mine hid their loot there.

"We will call it Clay's Lost Mine," one of them spreading this gossip in Chelsea's full of XXX seeing double.

"No, I liked Nathan's lost mine," another seeing triple.

"No, I will call it The Dutch Man's Lost Mine," the last and was ill over the other two so had the living daylights beaten out of him.

And an ape man who never made it home to Alaska had overheard, and he walked funny down High Street as was an ape, a lot bigger than a chimpanzee, and the ape smashed a toy shop window open, and rode away on a brand-new tricycle, a plastic bucket and shovel as well, he was away to find that mine and be rich.

And an alarm in the busted toy shop went off and girls in black appeared, the new order in Terlingua, with sniffer dogs, long fangs and dogs and girls deliberately not given daily meals to make them ferocious, yes that ape man better pedal hard.

An American Howling was coming up behind his moons.

THE END

ABOUT THE AUTHOR

Keith Hulse

Keith was an archaeologist, soldier, entrepreneur, Scottish War Blinded Veteran.
Stories come tumbling into my left temple and out the right ear.
Spirit people visit him, his house is full of cats, perhaps why.
There are illustrated and non illustrated versions of the books.

BOOKS BY THIS AUTHOR

Big Foot, A Betty Lou Sheriff Bottom Murder Mystery Comedy : Illustrated

Johnny Christy plays a mouth organ under a large sombrero, this man has a secret, he enters patrol vehicles unnoticed, while they are moving.
He is the secret agent in this tale of laughs.
The heroes are Sheriff Bottom and his Deputy Clay Eagle, hapless imbeciles.
But they get the job done not by their deeds but by luck and the efforts of others.
That mean they get the glory.
Yes, it does.
They are heroes.
They caught Big Foot and let it go.
So, who believes them, we do.
Plenty of Big Foot action.

Ghost Wife

74256 words, 159 pages, illustrated.
Oh, Morag dear, you died so do what ghosts do, Rest In Peace.
"Not on your Nelly, I am very much alive, and stop ogling the medium Con, dear." Plenty of madcap ridiculous fun. Information on the After Life.
Is comic mayhem, fanciful rubbish to tickle. The ghosts here will not haunt but make you laugh, so do not worry about holding bibles, these ghosts are clowns.

Ghost Romance, A Comedy Of Errors

54980 words, 218 words, illustrated.
A nonstop ghostly ridiculous adventure from Borneo to New York Zoo, with Calamity the orangutan in tow. So, load up on bananas and figs as the ape eats non-stop.
"Ouk," is her only word spoken.
Do not worry about the extras feeding the crocodiles, they come under a dime a dozen and are not in any union, and better, made of indigestible rubber.
Not to worry animal lovers, a vet is on standby by for the sweet crocodiles, sea water variety so bigger, nastier, fierce, and wanting you as food.
This book speaks heaps for food out there, a mixture of local, Indian, Chinese, Portuguese, Dutch, British, you name it, it found a way onto the menu.
Eat more than a banana and drink condensed tea milk to sweeten you up.

Eagor The Monster, A Laughing Tale

84488 words 248 pages
An epic book of giggles.
Aggressive comedy.
The humorous tale of an ugly monster who
cheats on his many girlfriends.
But he is so ugly?
He works for himself although signed up
to do jobs for the HOOD cousins.
Discount salespersons who will sell you what you
do not need, like BAD Granny who hunts were-wolfs
from her zoomed up mobile home.
A were-wolf girl with a pretty ankle who yes, is
one of the ugly monsters' girls.
Come laugh meeting Eagor's other friends,

Such as Badbladder who dresses as Bunnykins,
In his effort to marry Princess Lana.
And the monster treats his friends bad, as
gets Badbladder to do his job of pulling
twenty carts full of holidaying villagers on
The Blackhood express.
Giggle laugh snort meeting Eagor's enemies, Bear a chili
Addicted bear, Morag a frizzled-out witch, Wee Mary her
apprentice
and a Glasgow hard case who knows how to deal with Eagor,
"Will you marry me monster," as Wee Mary is desperate.
Just a funny silly tale to brighten your day.
All about magic to make you magically aware of life.

Coachman, A Travellers Laughing Melody

Ah, the sparkle is what the thieving pretty ankle beat out
Of Dwarf, which is his name and proud of it.
And she escapes to get as far away as the coach takes her.
Except the coach picks up passengers, Dwarf for one.
ALL AFTER THE SPARKLE for they covet wealth. Nothing wrong
with that, except when it involves nasty Grannies, were-wolfs,
cowboy sheriffs, Lancelot and an oily Mr. Oiler salesperson
related to the famous Hood Bros.
In this tale come escape to a parallel dimension and forget the
horrors of ours by laughing at the injustice Mr. Dwarf gets.
He is an object of slap stick, messy it be.

Wamba, Comedy Of Soldier Fools, And Rations

The hero is him on the horse.
Nothing nice about him as he is a Garrison Man who spends
nights in the establishment, 'Filthy Big bertha's.'
That says it all.
Every tale has a girl and she is rescued by him from fiends from
your nightmares, and just cannot get away from him.

He sleeps with his dog.
A loveable dog you do not want to adopt.
It has fleas so means so does he and now her.
A love story if ever there was one.
He adores her.
She hates him.
Nothing else to this clean-cut tale apart
from full of imbeciles and slap stick comedy.

Tiberius Grant

Grant Science Fiction
The Way
Starts as a trial
Transmigration of the soul
Ancient Celtic lore
The way is way of life
Anti-war
Love story
Tiberius the Ram
His loves
Evil of big business and owners, Presidents and Corrupt rulers.
Tiberius is for the protection of life, eco system, planets
to come our way.
Celtic and Mexican raided.

Mingo Drum Vercingetorix, Birdman

Birdman Mingo Drum Vercingetorix, Birdman, King of the
Artebrates,
Fighting aliens, Human, and amphibian Madrawt, for his home,
Planet Maponos.
Based on the history of ancient Gaul, and Native American
Indian Tribes, when they meet
A superior military machine.

No longer single heroic warrior combat.
This love story is a tearjerker but twists into a happy ending.

Mungo

Mungo 'Lady' or 'Mr.' just imagine these lion humanoids parading Californian beaches, were the beautiful folk resort. These lion people are nice looking and will soon have you ogling, to the jealousy of the other types loitering the warm sand.
Love jumps races and here species. Your siblings one day might bring an alien with a red Mohican hair style instead of the human heavy rock boy next door to dinner.
Here lizard folk ruled by queens, such as Carman hates humans, so adventure and war with her against Mungo, King of Lions.
And no one wins in a war as a human star ship arrives and enslaves the lot.
Advanced humans see other humans as undesirables, especially if a 'nutter' rides a lion .
These lizard folk like humans at a barbecue, as the burgers, steaks, and sausages.
No wonder Mungo wars against them. Well, we eat cows, sheep, pigs, and fish. That is what these lizards see humans as, dinner.
And an ape more like a mongoose and teddy bear.
and wide eyed too, is a sub story in the book called,
Mazarrats

The Man

A peek at predestination.
79586 words, 419 pages, illustrated.
Mammoth read.
Are we predestined, reborn?
Early Christian dogma had reincarnation as a core belief.
Until The Empress Theodora, A.D. 561 banned such an idea?
She wanted worshipped, declared divine and a bust next to Julius and prayed to.

Oh well, tar la, LA, such is life, those above make the rules.
So, The Man is reborn again to pass or fail his lessons, depending on if he shows mercy or not?
Meet his loves, Nesta whom he left on the spiritual plane.
Meet his friends, Tintagel the Clone who authored this book.
Meet The master Priest, a vampire firmly making this book a horror novel.
Meet aliens galore and realise we are not alone.
See the colours of space and wonder at the music of the stars.
Look and listen in The Man.

Ants 169

82652 words 169 illustrations. 262 pages
Mammoth adventure with Luke of The Ants, a rival to Tarzan, whereas Tarzan was brought up on ape milk, Luke is raised on Black Ant milk.
Luke dances to the unseen spiritual power of the universe for strength. When he shows compassion, mercy he glows, otherwise he walks in revenge, darkness.
Sound familiar.
Amazing strength and he battles Insect Nobles for the dominant species on Planet World.
Humanoid Insects from chromosome splicing.
Human genes into insects to make them taller, handsome, attractive but cruel masters of Planet World.
A good hero needs a side kick, Luke has Utna, a giant Black Ant he rides, saves shoe leather. Come ride a giant ant with Luke. Let the breeze refresh you.
Look at the crimson moons, fill with him 'spring fever' and you are too.
Spiritually moving as Luke like King David, dances to and grows with Spirit

Printed in Great Britain
by Amazon

30497268R00126